GRACE IS A
PRE-EXISTING CONDITION
FAITH, SYSTEMS, AND MENTAL HEALTHCARE

GRACE IS A
PRE-EXISTING CONDITION
FAITH, SYSTEMS, AND MENTAL HEALTHCARE

DAVID FINNEGAN-HOSEY

CHURCH
PUBLISHING
INCORPORATED

Church Publishing
19 East 34th Street
New York, NY 10016
www.churchpublishing.org

Cover design by Paul Soupiset
Typeset by Rose Design

A record of this book is available from the Library of Congress.

ISBN-13: 978-1-64065-196-8 (paperback)
ISBN-13: 978-1-64065-197-5 (ebook)

This book is dedicated to:
my godfather, Patrick,
who reminds me that grace came before me;
and my goddaughter, Miriam,
who reminds me that grace will continue after me.

Ad majorem Dei gloriam

Contents

Gratitude

In writing, in prayer, and in life, it is worth the time to begin with gratitude. This is a lesson I have been learning and re-learning ever since I was diagnosed with bipolar disorder, even and especially in painful circumstances or in times when, due to the realities of mental illness, the "feeling" or "attitude" of gratitude is difficult to come by. As I write this, I give thanks that at the moment the feeling of gratitude is in fact present. I am exceedingly grateful for so many people who have supported me and made this book possible and, even more than that, have made my life and my health possible.

Milton-Brasher Cunningham and the entire team at Church Publishing have enabled this project to come into being. Milton has been more than my editor—he's been an advocate, an encourager, and a friend. Paul Soupiset, who created the cover art for both this book and my previous one, is a wonderful artist whose designs reflect his deep reading of the authors who are lucky enough to work with him. I remain eternally grateful to Mike Stavlund for introducing me to Milton and Paul, and for helping with the launch of my first book in such a beautiful and personal way. I continue to give thanks, as well, for Teresa P. Mateus and Sarah Griffith Lund, who encouraged me to write the initial book proposal for *Christ on the Psych Ward*, without which this second book never would have come into being. Hailey Joy Scandrette made crucial contributions as my research assistant for this book, not only identifying helpful sources but offering insights and integrative connections which continue to inform my own understanding of the topic.

I give thanks for all of the teachers, instructors, and professors who have shaped my thinking over the years. In particular, my understanding of care in the context of systems is deeply influenced by Dr. Cedric C. Johnson, my pastoral care professor at Wesley Theological Seminary. Pieces of this book's third chapter were adapted from writing that I originally completed for Dr. Carla Works at Wesley. My experience of Clinical Pastoral Education at the National Institutes of Health in Bethesda, Maryland, under the instruction of the Rev. Ellen Swinford, was also influential in my writing.

I am grateful to my colleagues at Barton College who have been patient with me during the writing of this manuscript; and grateful for all of the students at Barton and in all of the other campus contexts in which I have been in ministry, from whom I have learned so much. The Rev. Bishop Valerie Melvin, my Regional Minister in the Christian Church in North Carolina (Disciples of Christ), has also been unfailingly supportive of my writing, advocacy, and ministry, for which I am deeply appreciative.

As I reference throughout this book, many of the ideas and encounters that I sought to expand upon in writing were the result of invitations from congregations, campuses, hospital staffs, community advocates, conference organizers, podcasters, journalists, professors, and festival organizers to share my story and reflect on my experiences. My thanks go out to all those who offered me the chance to "go first" with my story and who took on the courageous work of facilitating spaces for honest, difficult conversations about mental health struggle and recovery. I've appreciated the opportunity to share ideas with my fellow "Journey" bloggers of the Mental Health Network of the United Church of Christ. The Mental Health Track at the 2018 Summer Institute on Theology and Disability, facilitated by Drs. John Swinton and Warren Kinghorn, was also particularly helpful in allowing me to explore some of the material in this book. Thank you, as well, to all the other authors and artists who have graciously shared a microphone with me throughout these past two years—Dr. Tonya Armstrong, Chessy Prout, Mary Button, Rev. Rachael Keefe, and Dr. Alison Downie.

Books have a soundtrack. This book's soundtrack was provided by The Many, Brothers Bear, and mewithoutYou. Thanks to them, and to all of you making music that will serve as the soundtrack for other people's writing.

My family has been unflaggingly supportive of me, a gift not received by everyone with a mental illness. Many thanks to my parents, Marion and Gary; my sister, Anne, and brother-in-law, Scott;

and my mother-in-law, Jane, who in addition to being personally supportive has also become a mental health advocate in her own congregational setting. To Leigh, my wife—I think writing these books has been harder on you than it has on me, and without your encouragement, ideas, listening, and love, I would never have been able to finish this project. Our dog Penny Lane also provided vital editing and typing help.

And finally, I will end this hopelessly partial list of gratitudes by giving thanks to the One in whom all gratitude begins, whose grace precedes and transcends me. With every last breath in my lungs, I can only say, "Thank You. Thank You. Thank You."

Starting with Grace

Three Stories

I'll begin with three stories. Or, more accurately, I'll begin with three different versions of the same story, like swimming in a river that seems slow and placid on its surface, but conceals a complex swirl of currents of different speeds and strengths, the surface serenity an oversimplified illusion and yet nonetheless beautiful, somehow revealing of an essential truth.

The first story goes like this. In 2011, after finishing my first year of seminary studies with the goal of becoming a parish pastor, I, with the help of some friends, admitted myself into the psychiatric unit of a local hospital. It was a scary experience, and also, I needed to be somewhere where I was safe, where the swirling thoughts that had grabbed hold of my brain's steering wheel couldn't drive me right off a cliff. I was in that hospital unit for a few weeks, and then was released, and then went back in, and out, and in, and out, and finally ended up in a longer-term rehabilitation facility, where I received a diagnosis of type II bipolar disorder, which seemed to more accurately reflect that jagged experience I was having. With this diagnosis came medicines that helped me find some steady ground to stand on in the midst of the overwhelming currents of my out-of-order emotions, and therapies that gave me some hope of coping and survival, at least day by day by day. I returned home, which at the time was Washington, D.C., and while things were still really hard for a really long time, I started to share my story; slowly at first, hesitantly, awkwardly.

I began to realize that by going first with my own story of mental health struggle, mental illness, and long path to recovery, I could help create space for others to share their own stories and particularly to empower faith communities to be places where people could bring their whole selves to God and each other, could be brave and vulnerable and honest about their struggles in a space where such sharing could be met with care and grace and solidarity. This story-sharing eventually led to the opportunity to write a book about my experiences[1] and more opportunities to share and create space for vital conversations about mental health in faith communities, festival grounds, seminary classrooms, and hospitals.

This is still a hard story for me to tell. It's about an excruciating time in my life. There are times when I still balk or hesitate to tell it. And yet I am grateful for the opportunity to tell it, and am passionate about the way in which this "going first" creates spaces for conversations that we need to be having. This story, at least on its placid surface, is one of redemption and healing, in which a much healthier version of me is able to look back on a difficult time and share about it in a way that offers hope to others who are struggling. I like this version of myself, this story of myself.

Here is a second version of the story, a different current flowing underneath its surface. During that time in Washington, D.C., that really-long-really-hard time, when I was beginning to tell my story and to heal, I learned that I had what insurance companies refer to as a pre-existing condition. My insurance claims for my multiple hospitalizations were denied. I found myself, at the age of twenty-seven, in major medical debt—more debt than I had ever experienced. Having lived through a major mental health crisis, I discovered that the most significant mental health challenge I would face was dealing with the mental healthcare system, with all it entails: bills and hours on the phone with big insurance companies, impersonal institutions with no care for the impact their policies have on actual people, debt, debt collectors, gaps in coverage, inequities and lack of parity in access to care. This story, this struggle, complicated the too-easy narrative of past crisis and present healing, even as I was learning how to share that first story. Redemption and recovery were complicated, not only by

---

1. David Finnegan-Hosey, *Christ on the Psych Ward* (New York: Church Publishing, 2018).

the ongoing and chronic nature of my condition but by the constant reality of economic systems and political discourses, of whose impact on my life I was suddenly aware.

That I was caught off-guard by this impact, rather than being aware of it as a background reality of my whole life, is a result not only of my naivete but also of societal injustice, the unearned privilege afforded to me by a system that had, up until then, been built for me at the expense of others—the poor, communities of color, LGBTQ folks, women whose pregnancies or whose experiences of sexual assault were treated as "pre-existing conditions."

This injustice leads me to my third version of the story, swirling under the surface during that same really-long-really-hard time. I was in a psychologist's office, shifting uncomfortably in a comfortable chair. Everything seemed soft: soft chairs, soft lighting, and, somehow, the soft sound of water flowing. The psychologist introduced me to the concepts of Dialectical Behavior Therapy. At some point in the conversation she looked up from her desk. "You know," she said—her voice, too, was soft—"I don't often have men in these groups."

"Oh," I replied, "that's interesting. Why is that?"

"Most men with your diagnosis end up in jail," she said, matter-of-factly.

I didn't know what to say. I was learning that mass incarceration and chronic homelessness have replaced a functioning mental health-care system for most people with mental illnesses in this country. I was learning that my experience of mental illness and mental healthcare was still a relatively privileged one. For many people in this country, the safety and road to recovery I had begun to walk was a distant fantasy because of a lack of access to care, a lack of economic means, or a complicated history of various ways that the mental healthcare system had contributed to, rather than alleviated, the discriminatory treatment of various communities.

As I began to share my story with congregations, students, and groups of pastors and chaplains, I hoped that by "going first" and modeling a healthy vulnerability I would be able to help create spaces where difficult stories and conversations could be shared, stories and conversations that had previously been silenced behind a wall of stigma and shame. I have found that this way of sharing stories has, in fact, been helpful for many. At the same time, I have become increasingly aware that my story is a single story, and not a universal story of mental illness.[2]

My story, even with all of the pain and brokenness it includes, is a relatively privileged one. Starting with my story, then, has its limitations. Most prominently, it does not touch on or communicate all of the various struggles faced by people with mental health problems in the United States. In fact, many of the most difficult and important conversations around mental health—questions around homelessness, incarceration, and violence; questions around race, gender, and sexuality; questions about veteran mental health—don't get highlighted when I share my own story. My story, in other words, reveals, and it also conceals. So, I started naming the single story at the beginning of all of my talks, and saying that a single story needs to be the beginning of the conversation about mental healthcare in this country, not the end of it.

As I've shared my story, I have heard from many different people, with many different stories. I have heard people in rural communities talk about the almost total lack of mental health resources, including a lack of hospital beds and units for people with psychiatric needs, and the harsh comorbidity of addiction, mental illness, and situational despair. I have heard from people who struggle to destigmatize psychiatric medication because of real experiences and concerns about medication being abusively administered as a means of control, in settings such as prisons, group homes, and in detention centers caging children at the border, rather than as a means of healing. I have heard from people working in marginalized communities where the history of abuse and misuse exacerbates mental health stigma. I have heard from people who are tired of chronic homelessness and mass incarceration standing in for a functioning mental health system. I heard from pastors and church staff who are stretched beyond their training and abilities trying

---

2. See Chimamanda Adichie, "The danger of a single story," *TED*, July 2009, available online: *https://www.ted.com/talks/chimamanda_adichie_the_danger_of_a_single_story.*

to fill in the gaps in a broken system. I heard from people with their own mental health challenges who struggle every day and who long for the support of their faith community, their friends, and their family. And I've heard from family members, friends, and church members who long to offer support but aren't sure where to start.

To navigate this world as someone with a mental illness is to simultaneously engage in multiple conversations. The (often internal) conversation with the voice of illness itself is persistently exhausting. I have elected to join the communal conversation in order to break the silence and challenge the stigma around mental health struggles. The broader, public conversation impacts those of us with mental illnesses through no choice of our own. It's a conversation about us, and often without us. I choose to be involved in that conversation, to insert myself into it with a loud insistence when necessary, because I have some buffer against some of its most harmful currents, and because otherwise I find myself being talked about with no voice of my own, no contribution.

This latter public conversation impacts people with mental illnesses in multiple and unequal ways. Those sleeping under the bridge. Those in jail instead of sitting in a comfortable psychologist's office. The victims of school shootings still to come because people with mental illnesses are scapegoated in exchange for silence around guns, gender, and white supremacy. These people are all hurt and marginalized by this public conversation. We need to have a better conversation. It's time those of us in faith communities thought more deeply, more faithfully, and spiritually about the impact this public conversation has on the souls of people who grapple with a difficult internal struggle.

The mental health system in this country is exactly that: a system. Mental illness and mental health challenges are not solely individual struggles, but are systems issues as well. And where there are systems, there are powers and principalities to be named and challenged.

There is also grace. Grace which offers the hope for transformation and wholeness. The mental health system in the United States alienates many of its participants, and excludes many others. But the faithful response to alienation is not despair. It is, rather, the sharing of grace. Grace precedes harmful and unjust systems. By grace, creation, including humanity, is called into being. We are created with gracious intent, made for community, for connection, and for care. Systems come later. Grace comes before. Grace goes first.

As I began to address some of these overlapping conversations in my talks, I heard something else that dawned on me slowly at first. I began to hear the ways in which our supposedly secular language about mental healthcare in this country is surprisingly (and unconsciously) spiritual, even theological.

Why Thinking Theologically Matters

I am a person with theological training whose work is in the field of spiritual and pastoral care. The fact that I see the language of theology in our healthcare debates is, perhaps, a case of having a hammer and only seeing nails. But what I saw is more than a personal bias. The terms in which I found myself gaining an imposed proficiency— pre-existing, insurance, debt, universal—had profound resonances with the Christian theological lexicon. The connections were at times overt, at other times hidden, but ever present.

When I first began noticing these resonances, I thought this would be a book about how our vocabulary of mental healthcare grew from a seedbed of theological soil. The goal, then, would be to engage in the theological task of making healthier soil. I have decided, however, that I am rather agnostic as to the particular order of source and product, chicken and egg. Does our healthcare vocabulary arise from theological language, or is our theological language formed by the social, economic, and cultural realities of our country? Does the idea create the material, or does the material create the idea? Theologian Walter Wink describes the interplay: "Neither [the inner or outer] pole is the cause of the other. Both come into existence together and cease to exist together."[3] I am interested in these resonances, and

---

3. Walter Wink, *The Powers*, vol. 1: *Naming the Powers: The Language of Power in the New Testament* (Philadelphia: Fortress Press, 1984), 5.

the ways in which they reveal how we as a society speak about what matters most to us. This language, I hope to show, is inherently theological, whether we realize it or not, whether we profess a particular religious belief or not. It is worth bringing the language of theology to bear on the crisis of mental healthcare in the United States because these systems with their surprisingly theological language also have surprisingly detrimental effects on the spirit, the soul, of the people impacted by them.

One might rightfully protest that our country is not a "Christian" country. The non-establishment of religion by the state is enshrined (itself a religious term) in our Constitution. We are a pluralistic nation in which the fastest growing religious group is those who choose not to identify with any particular religious group at all. Yet Christian belief—or at least something wearing the costume of Christian belief—has an outsized impact on our lives together. Leaving aside for a moment the overt ways in which religious rhetoric plays a role in our public life and the attempts by some to claim that the United States is, in fact, a "Christian nation," I want to uncover a deeper layer in this conversation.

Underneath our public discourse lie deeply held views about the world and our place in it that cannot help but shape our actions and our policies. Those beliefs, whether overtly Christian or not, are a form of faith, what Sharon Daloz Parks defines as "meaning-making in its most comprehensive dimensions." "In other words, whenever we organize our sense of a particular object, a series of activities, or an institution, we are also compelled to compose our sense of its place in the whole of existence."[4] Our institutions, our systems, are connected to our faith, our deepest and broadest understanding of the world in which we exist.

In a sense, institutions and systems—including the mental health system—have what we might call an "embedded theology," a deep-level way of thinking about the nature of reality that often goes

---

4. Sharon Daloz Parks, *Big Questions Worthy Dreams: Mentoring Emerging Adults in Their Search for Meaning, Purpose, and Faith*, rev. ed. (San Francisco: Jossey-Bass, 2011), 28.

unexamined and unarticulated. In their book *How to Think Theologically*, Howard W. Stone and James O. Duke distinguish between "embedded theology," which is "the understanding(s) of faith disseminated by the church and assimilated by its members in their daily lives," and "deliberative theology," which is "a process of reflecting on multiple understandings of the faith implicit in the life and witness of Christians in order to identify and/or develop the most adequate understanding possible." They add: "Our embedded theology may seem so natural and feel so comfortable that we carry it within us for years, unquestioned and perhaps even unspoken except when we join in the words of others at worship. . . . Deliberative reflection questions what had been taken for granted."[5] Stone and Duke are speaking here, specifically, of Christian theological reflection. But if we take Daloz Parks's definition of faith ("meaning-making in its most comprehensive dimension") and combine it with the oft-referenced definition of theology as "faith seeking understanding," we begin to see how not only Christian communities but institutions and societies as a whole can have "embedded theologies"—ways of making meaning that are ensconced and often unexamined. Illnesses are constituted as pre-existing conditions that lead to denials of care. Uninsured individuals rack up massive medical debt. Mental illnesses are inaccurately associated with interpersonal violence. These realities grow out of the soil of meaning-making systems, often hidden in darkness. I hope to shed some light: to reveal the space that often exists between our embedded systemic theology and a theology based on the activity of God's grace, and to call us all, together, toward healthier ways of thinking about healthcare—mental healthcare, yes, and healthcare in general. The brokenness of our healthcare system has spiritual impacts that restrict or block the creative flow of grace that is God's original intent for the world, which reveals a spiritual component, a faith component, to efforts to fix the brokenness of this system, so that grace may more freely flow.

---

5. Howard W. Stone and James O. Duke, *How to Think Theologically*, 3rd ed. (Minneapolis: Fortress Press, 2013), 18.

Grace Came First

What do I mean by grace? Grace is the unconditional love offered by God because such self-giving is the essence, the very nature, of God. When I say grace is the love of God, I don't just mean a sort of nice feeling of love. Grace is a love that welcomes, that reconciles, and that transforms. And grace is a pre-existing condition. It is, I would argue, the truly pre-existing condition of all humankind, even of all creation. Grace is prior to what we do and what we say. It existed before bipolar disorder. It existed before words—words about politics, words about mental illness, words about me. It came before us. Grace was, and is. Grace creates us, grace forms us, grace breathes life into us. Grace is the original intention, the creative and unitive force, that goes before everything.

To speak of grace as a "condition" might be verbally and theologically jarring, at first. Isn't it more of a process, an activity, initiated by God? When I name grace as a pre-existing condition, what I mean is that grace is the original state of creation, the foundational reality on which our existence is presupposed and from which it arises. Frederick Buechner says:

> The grace of God means something like: Here is your life. You might never have been, but you *are* because the party wouldn't have been complete without you. Here is the world. Beautiful and terrible things will happen. Don't be afraid. I am with you. Nothing can ever separate us. It's for you I created the universe. I love you.[6]

We are breathed into being, formed, by grace. Nothing to be done about that. But what we can do, what we are quite stunningly capable of doing, is get in the way of grace, restricting and blocking the channels by which divine love flows in and through us. When we refuse to listen to people who are sick and suffering, people struggling with cancer or mental illness or diabetes or chronic pain, people who have been targeted by violence or abuse or oppression, we block grace. When we

---

6. Frederick Buechner, *Wishful Thinking: A Seeker's ABC*, rev. and exp. ed. (San Francisco: HarperSanFrancisco, 1993), 39.

shut down our inherent capacity for empathy and connection, see people as problems to be solved, sickness as personal failure, suffering as moral inferiority, we block grace.

People are not problems. Sickness is not failure. Suffering is not immorality. When we cut off grace—when we purposefully block the pre-existing rhythms of creation and compassion—that is a problem. That is a failure. That is immorality. That is sin. Choosing to hurt people, to reject people's stories, to refuse care for people is a choice. We do that. But we don't have to. We can make different choices. We were made for love, for empathy, for connection, for the sharing of stories because grace came first. Grace is a pre-existing condition.

While the imagining of a gracious God flows throughout the Bible[7], the language of grace emerges most fully in the writings of the apostle Paul and those writings that, while their authorship is debated by scholars, are attributed to the Pauline tradition. I want to focus in on one of those latter writings in particular, as it provides one of the most succinct examples of the language of grace that has influenced Christian theology, particularly Protestant theology.

"For by grace you have been saved through faith, and this is not your own doing; it is the gift of God—not the result of works, so that no one may boast" (Ephesians 2:8–9). These two verses summarize Paul's[8] language of grace that has so influenced the Christian understanding of salvation. Here, two of the core principles of the Protestant Reformation—*solo fide*, by faith alone, and *solo gratia*, by grace alone—seem to emerge in crystal clarity. But these verses, like any short quotation, are pulled from a broader context that fleshes out their full meaning. They are part of a wider story. The author continues on in

---

7. It is a common misconception, shaped by centuries of Christian anti-Semitism, that the God of the Old Testament is a God of wrath while the God of the New Testament is a God of grace. This is, in fact, an ancient heresy, condemned by the early church, known as Marcionism. The Old Testament, or Hebrew Bible, is filled with language around God's *chesed*—steadfast love and covenant loyalty—to God's people, a relationship always initiated by God and healed by God.

8. There is not space here to delve into the scholarly debates over the authorship of Ephesians. Suffice to say that, whoever the author, the letter uses the language of, is consistent with, and expands upon earlier Pauline writing on the topic of grace.

the next verse, "For we are what God has made us, created in Christ Jesus for good works, which God prepared beforehand to be our way of life" (2:10). We are created, in the grace referred to by this formative summation, to work for the common good, something prepared by God beforehand; something, in other words, that pre-existed us, and all of creation. Grace, somehow, saves us in a way that our own striving and self-justification cannot. And yet, at the same time, what grace saves us for is apparently a life of working for good, which is the thing we were originally created to do. This passage draws the connection between the Christian theological claim that all creation is through Christ, the saving activity of grace, and the work to which we are called.

If we expand our lens to the broader passage, an even wider story emerges, particularly if, with some help, we navigate our way through the tangled web of translation from the biblical Greek. We find that grace saves us from powerful things with names like "ruler" and "authority" and "power" and "dominion" (Ephesians 1:21). A more modern word to describe these ancient concepts might be "systems." Grace saves us from systems that cause harm for a life of working for the common good, which in turn is a life working to change systems that cause harm. The wider story of this passage from Ephesians is that we are saved *by* pre-existing grace, *from* unhealthy systems, *for* the common good.

A Wider Grace

This book is an attempt to widen my single story of mental health struggle into a broader conversation about mental healthcare systems and, even wider, into a conversation about the grace that saves us, in the context of broken systems, for the good of all. It is not necessarily a book about healthcare policy, nor a how-to guide for organizing, though resources on both of these topics will be referenced throughout. It is an exploration of the resonances between the language of theology and the struggle for care that is more accessible and just.

Throughout the book, you will find reflections on personal experience, theological understandings, and ministry practices. These are three lenses I bring to this conversation, three different threads that weave in and out of each other. These threads are aspects of myself that I can't help but bring to my writing. As someone with a mental illness who encounters the reality of the way this world treats people like me, my personal narrative weaves in and out of everything I write on this topic. As a person of faith, specifically someone who finds my home within the Protestant Christian faith tradition, I bring a particular theological lens and manner of theological reflection to this work. While I hope that this book will be of help not solely to those who share this tradition with me, it is the place from which I begin. As a person whose vocational calling and daily work is in the practice of ministry, specifically of chaplaincy—in other words, working at the intersection of the church with other spheres of daily life—one of my primary motivations is practical reflection on the ministry the church can be doing in the world and the way we can be doing it.

In these pages, I hope you will find an underlying movement of grace. That grace often reveals itself precisely at the places where grace would seem to be blocked by indifference, policy, or pain. While humans are capable of getting in the way of grace, grace is even more capable of slipping through the cracks in our walls and sneaking around our obstacles to invite new growth. Grace came before these thoughts and these words. Grace is, I believe, the precondition that allows for their existence, and will, I pray, work through and correct their flaws. Grace will continue on, too, long after these words, leading us ever onward and ever homeward.

PART

1

Beginnings

We are saved *by* pre-existing grace,
from unhealthy systems,
for the common good.

What is a pre-existing condition? What might it mean to say that grace is pre-existing? Or, for that matter, that grace is a condition at all? And what does being saved mean anyway? The insistence in Ephesians 2, among other places in the New Testament, that we have been saved by grace has often been interpreted in ways that are both individualistic (salvation is for *me*) and entirely spiritualized (salvation has to do with where my incorporeal soul goes after death, and is a separate matter from my embodied existence on this side of eternity). Yet the letter to the church in Ephesus is an inherently social document, that addresses concrete and embodied divisions within a community and understands salvation not as individualistic and future-focused but as a present and cosmic reality for the whole church.

New Testament scholar Dr. Mitzi J. Smith says "Ephesians reads like a legal document detailing a corporate merger of two major bodies"—Jewish and Gentile Christ-followers—and the letter's reference to "God's elevation of Christ assumes a this-worldly (present and future) and political maneuver." From the lens of a contemporary African American reader, she argues, the content of the letter offers assurance that "the power of God is greater than the legal and political powers wielded by the authors and supporters of . . . political agendas that threaten to erode our civil rights."[1] Dr. E. Elizabeth Johnson

---

1. Mitzi J. Smith, "Ephesians," in *True to Our Native Land: An African American New Testament Commentary*, ed. Brian K. Blount et al. (Minneapolis: Fortress, 2007), 348–352.

writes that the letter's quotation of the earlier Pauline slogan, "by grace you have been saved," represents a developing understanding of salvation as a present reality and "the church as a heavenly as well as earthly reality," into which Christians have been raised with Christ.[2]

Whatever the author of Ephesians means by salvation by grace, then, it is a reality with implications, not only for an individual in the future, but for a community in the here and now. Salvation is inclusive of healing, wholeness, and liberation in relation to the economic, social, and embodied realities of those in need of God's grace—all of us.

---

2. E. Elizabeth Johnson, "Ephesians," in *Women's Bible Commentary: Revised and Updated,* 3rd ed., ed. Carol A. Newsom, Sharon H. Ringe, and Jacqueline E. Lapsley (Louisville: Westminster John Knox, 2012), 577.

1

What's Pre-existing, and What Isn't

I remember when I first learned I had a pre-existing condition.

I was living in a basement apartment in Northeast D.C. It was a dark, damp, dank place. I was in desperate need of housing when I got out of the hospital, and friends offered me the room at the last minute. They had hoped to stop renting it out because it was not a particularly livable space, but I was in need and they had a room, so they reluctantly agreed to rent it to me. For six months after my stay in a Connecticut hospital, I struggled to wake up in the morning, with little to no natural light touching my makeshift bedroom. I was home, and I was trying to heal, and it was still hard, and all was not well. During this time, I started to learn that navigating this country's mental healthcare system, or its lack thereof, was as much of a challenge to one's mental health as mental illness itself.

My hands shook as I read the notice. My eyes blurred. I couldn't register what the letter was saying. My insurance claims for my hospitalizations were rejected. In addition to grappling with the identity crisis of my new diagnosis, I was now tens of thousands of dollars in debt. All because the insurance company had deemed my bipolar disorder to be a pre-existing condition. Not long after that, I lost my coverage entirely because my graduate school stopped offering student insurance. Applications for new insurance coverage came back with the same answer: denied due to pre-existing condition. Prior to the passage of the Affordable Care Act in 2010, and the phasing in of its major provisions in 2014, insurers in the United States were within their legal rights to deny coverage to people with a whole host of medical issues; my diagnosis of bipolar disorder was just one of them. At the age of twenty-six, I had more medical costs than I'd ever had in my life, and no insurance coverage to help defray them. The debt, and the potential for future costs, weighed on me. I was scared.

In 2011, when a doctor first told me that the awful experience I was having might be a mental illness, the diagnosis came as a relief. I am a person of words, a person whose sense of purpose, whose vocation has always been caught up in a love of words. I write stories, I sing songs, I preach sermons, I study theology—*theo-logos*: words about God. To hurt without words was, is, terrifying for me. Some people hate the label of a mental illness diagnosis, and I understand the resistance to a simple, narrow label. But me? I was relieved to have words.

I know now that my relief was naïve. I didn't know, then, that bipolar disorder constituted a "pre-existing condition," which allowed insurance companies to categorically deny my applications for coverage. Over and over again. Of course, my prior indifference to this reality was privilege, plain and simple. The maladies considered to be pre-existing conditions are legion, and innumerable are those possessed of them. I was shielded from this particular thorn in the side until my mid-twenties; most Americans are not so lucky. Almost none of us can hope to escape our conditions being deemed as pre-existing, at least not forever. Cancer, complications during pregnancy, mental health challenges, long-term effects of injuries, all hover just around the corner, and all signified a slide into a potentially disastrous chasm of denied coverage. Some of us can escape illness or hospitalization some of the time. None of us can escape it all of the time.

For me, the 2014 phasing in of the Affordable Care Act— "Obamacare"—was a major relief. The legislation had plenty of flaws. It was not the healthcare system I thought our country ultimately needed or ought to have, but it provided me with some protection, with some right to parity for my mental health conditions, and with some right to coverage in spite of my diagnosis. Its expansion of Medicaid (adopted by only thirty-six states and the District of Columbia) allowed me to afford healthcare even as a student, and its extension of coverage to those with pre-existing conditions allowed me to buy private insurance after I graduated from seminary in 2015.

I watched in frustration as a certain faction in Congress attempted, over and over again, to overturn the bill while failing to present a viable proposal that would offer me the same hope as the ACA. Then the 2016 election rolled around, and in 2017 a newly empowered anti-ACA faction in Congress dedicated themselves to "repeal and replace"—read, mainly repeal—Obamacare. Even as I write this chapter, the current administration is supporting action in federal courts to end the ACA, including its protections for people with pre-existing conditions.[1] When I hear reports about threats to these protections, the fear and anxiety I felt when I first read that letter from the insurance company come rushing back. It makes me scared. And it makes me angry.

At first, the immediate practical aspects of having a pre-existing condition weighed most heavily on me. I realized that not only had my initial hospital insurance claims been rejected but also that I would be unable to apply for new insurance coverage—a terrifying thought, given that, at that point, it was still unclear to me whether I would need to go back to the hospital.

I would. Repeatedly.

The rejection of the insurance claims from my initial hospitalization left me in a massive load of debt. This debt also weighed on me. At the time, it was difficult for me to talk with friends about any other topic; I was consumed by fear, anxiety, and scarcity. Pragmatic concerns dogged me, but as time wore on there was also a noticeable psychological and spiritual component to my pre-existing condition. Something about the label bothered me at a deeper level. Having an illness that is classified as a pre-existing condition felt like a stain on my being. It was a stain that questioned my purity and cleanliness as I approached the altar of resources of the mental healthcare system. It also carried with it a deeper, socially stigmatized stain.

---

1. Abby Goodnough, "Appeals Court Appears Skeptical About Constitutionality of Obamacare Mandate," *New York Times*, July 9, 2019, available online: *https://www.nytimes.com/2019/07/09/health/obamacare-appeals-court.html*.

To have a pre-existing condition is to be told you have a disease or a disorder that is somehow more severe than the "normal" things a human being encounters over the course of a year, or a lifetime. Having a pre-existing condition moved me, not only practically but socially, into the category of the "mentally ill." To have a pre-existing condition and to be rejected, therefore, from the provision of care that a "normal" or healthy person might have, was to face social stigmatization: a blight, a spot, on my very existence. It was a difficult adjustment.

I came to hate the term pre-existing condition, unable to say it without a wry turn of my mouth and a bitterness in my tone. In its deeper, stigmatizing impact I began to see a spiritual component, a layer of meaning—a harmful meaning—that dwelt underneath the surface of our day-to-day lives. A pre-existing condition carries a spiritual, as well as a medical, weight.

The Origins (and the Heresy) of Pre-existing Conditions

It's surprisingly difficult to figure out when the term "pre-existing condition" entered the medical insurance lexicon, but it seems to have first appeared in public discourse around the same time that the modern U.S. health insurance system began to take shape in the 1940s. [2] With the passing of the 1942 Stabilization Act during World War II, which limited wages in an effort to prevent inflation, private employers began offering insurance plans to attract employees. While this benefit was one that was initially popular for workers in an era of stagnant wages, it meant that, as the question of responsibility for healthcare began to come into national focus, it was defined in privatized terms. This was, literally, the creation of a "works-based" approach to healthcare, in which the burden of coverage was explicitly placed on

---

2. I owe this insight into the link between the 1942 Stabilization Act and the popularization of the term "pre-existing condition" to Hailey Joy Scandrette, who worked as my research assistant during the writing of this book. You can read some of her writing here: *https://haileyjs.wordpress.com/*.

the individual, either through their place of employment or their ability to pay for care outside of an employer-based system.

In this approach, care for the health of citizens was considered neither a right nor a gift, but rather something that had to be earned through work. Health then, unlike Paul's understanding of salvation, was implicitly something brought about by our own doing, the result of our own works. This might seem an odd comparison, but the New Testament language for "salvation" and "healing" is in fact deeply connected.

It is also worth noting that this shift to employer-based insurance took place during World War II—a time of national emergency. That this wartime system became the dominant means of healthcare coverage in the United States is one small piece of what the Poor People's Campaign refers to as "the War Economy," an economic system based on an assumption of perpetual crisis and war.[3]

Since then, the history of the U.S. healthcare system has been a series of piecemeal or stalled efforts at reform and expansion.[4] Significant efforts to fill in the gaps in the employer-based insurance system, such as the creation of Medicare and Medicaid under the Social Security Act in 1965, still fell short of universal access to care. Massive gaps in coverage remained. The Affordable Care Act continued this trend, filling some of the gaps in coverage, but maintaining the dominance of private insurance. Attempts to include a public, government-run insurance option failed to gain traction in Congress, while the expansion of Medicaid was rejected by many states. Prior to the ACA, private insurance companies had essentially unrestricted power to determine what constituted a pre-existing condition, a situation that could once again become the reality if the ACA ceases to be the law of the land.[5]

---

3. Poor People's Campaign, "A Moral Agenda Based on Fundamental Rights—War Economy and Militarism," *https://www.poorpeoplescampaign.org/demands/*.

4. For a good and (relatively) brief overview of reform efforts, see "Timeline: A History of Health Reform in the U.S.," created by the Kaiser Family Foundation and available online at: *https://www.kff.org/wp-content/uploads/2011/03/5-02-13-history-of-health-reform.pdf*.

5. Donna Rosato, "What Exactly Is a Pre-Existing Condition Anyway?," *Consumer Reports*, May 12, 2017, available online: *https://www.consumerreports.org/health-insurance/what-is-a-pre-existing-condition-anyway/*.

Parity of coverage for mental health and substance abuse disorders only existed in the law prior to the ACA as recently as 2008, and that legal requirement of parity did not cover individual marketplace plans until the ACA was passed.[6] In a sense, the healthcare system in the United States has been unable to escape the "original sin" of a privatized, employer-based, and for-profit health insurance system that first emerged, not as a long-term plan for the nation's overall health, but as a response to wartime crisis.

Around the same time as this emergence of what became the modern American health insurance system, the use of the term "pre-existing" came into popular usage as a way to describe health conditions. According to the Oxford English Dictionary, the first in-print use of the term in relation to healthcare coverage was in a 1947 article in a Nevada newspaper, the *Reno Evening Gazette*.[7] "Pre-existing" itself, on the other hand, has existed in its participle form for a long time: the Oxford English Dictionary's earliest citation of it in print is from a 1585 work titled *The Difference Betwene the Auncient Phisicke, First Taught by the Godly Forefathers*, where the word had overtly theological connotations: "God, which of nothing, that is hauing no matter, pre-existing, or goying before, hast created al the world."[8]

The theological meaning of the word "pre-existing," then, pre-existed the medical connotation of the term in the English language by around 350 years. Yet if we use the term "pre-existing" in a sentence in 2019, it's likely people—at least in the United States—will assume you

---

6. Kirsten Beronio, Rosa Po, Laura Skopec, and Sherry Glied, "Affordable Care Act Expands Mental Health and Substance Use Disorder Benefits and Federal Parity Protections for 62 Million Americans," U.S. Department of Health and Human Services, February 20, 2013, available online: *https://aspe.hhs.gov/report/affordable-care-act-expands-mental-health-and-substance-use-disorder-benefits-and-federal-parity-protections-62-million-americans*.

7. Oxford English Dictionary citation referenced by Patricia T. O'Conner and Stewart Kellerman, "Preexisting Conditions," *The Grammarphobia Blog*, July 27, 2012, available online: *https://www.grammarphobia.com/blog/2012/07/preexisting-conditions.html*.

8. O'Conner and Kellerman, "Preexisting Conditions," *The Grammarphobia Blog*.

are talking about health conditions. The healthcare connotation of the term has largely eclipsed its theological roots. This is not to say that the medical usage is in any way intentionally theological, of course; it is the language of risk management. And yet, the question of what is allowed to be considered pre-existing is a core piece of the Christian story and of Christian identity. Some of the earliest debates that shaped the development of Christian theology had to do with the concept of pre-existence. Though it wasn't exactly disease that was being debated, the concept of "original sin" does play into Christian understandings of un-health. But the early church had a deep sense that messing up the question of what was, and wasn't, pre-existing was a form of heresy.

"There Was a Time When He Was Not"

In the first few centuries after Jesus of Nazareth walked as a human on the earth, the Christian movement was a small community, largely defining itself in relation to the Judaism from which it emerged, and ostracized and often persecuted by the Roman Empire. But as time progressed, Christianity became more mainstream, and debates within Christianity began to affect the society at large. When the Emperor Constantine interfered in intra-Christian debates to secure imperial tranquility, it marked the first time the Christian church was required to codify its doctrine. Prior to this time, Christian faith had spread by word of mouth and developed into the oral traditions of the diverse communities that comprised the early church. The earliest literature in the New Testament consists of pastoral letters written to particular communities who already held to a diversity of traditions and practices and vocabularies for proclaiming their faith. By the end of the first century, these oral traditions about Jesus began to be written down, in different ways by distinct communities, giving us the differing accounts that today we refer to as the Gospels.

For about three hundred years after the death of Jesus, this diversity of communities with a shared story passed on the particular language and tradition unique to each group. These communities relied not on a set doctrine but rather something church historians refer to as

the "Rule of Faith," a brief summary of Christian belief with some vari-
ance between different communities.[9] The Judaism out of which the
early church emerged had the Shema, the core declaration of the faith
of Israel recorded in Deuteronomy 6:4: "Hear, O Israel: The Lord is
our God, the Lord alone. You shall love the Lord your God with all
your heart, and with all your soul, and with all your might." But the
church had not yet settled on such a succinct or unified declaration of
its faith. Instead, different communities had different ways of express-
ing the core Christian proclamation. We see hints of this diversity of
expressions of the Rule of Faith throughout the New Testament. For
example, in the second chapter of his letter to the church in Philippi,
Paul quotes what many scholars refer to as the "Christ hymn"—a proclamation in song of the Rule of Faith. The closing of Matthew's Gospel contains an early Trinitarian formula linked to the teaching and
formation of Christian disciples. What such proclamations had in
common was an emerging vocabulary of faith: the authority of Jesus
over and against the authority of the Roman Empire; a Trinitarian
understanding of God as a relational unity-in-community of Parent,
Child, and Spirit; and a set of ethics or norms for the behavior of the
people who would be called Christian.

The Emperor Constantine's decision to intervene in intra-
Christian debates forced the early church to structure its beliefs in a
more formal way. And the debate that swirled around Constantine's
decision to call the first "Ecumenical Council" was centered on how
Christians make sense of the pre-existence of Christ.

Both parties to the debate, it should be noted, believed in the
pre-existence of the Divine Word or *logos*, referenced in the first verses
of John's Gospel, prior to the Incarnation of that Word in Jesus of
Nazareth; what was at stake was whether this divine Word was *created*
by God, or whether it was pre-existent with God prior to creation.[10]
Were the Father and the Son together at creation, or did the Father

9. Justo L. González, *Essential Theological Terms* (Louisville: Westminster John
Knox, 2005), 153.

10. Justo L. González, *The Story of Christianity*, vol. 1: *The Early Church to the
Dawn of the Reformation* (San Francisco: HarperSanFrancisco, 1984), 161.

first create the Son, and then the rest of creation? A popular priest in the city of Alexandria named Arius argued that the Son was created by God. While the debate may seem irredeemably esoteric to contemporary believers, at the time it was a matter of much popular interest. "Having a genius for propaganda, Arius set his favorite slogan to a popular tune, and soon half of Alexandria was singing, 'There was a time when the Son was not.'"[11] The controversy crept into public discourse to such an extent that one theologian of the time, Gregory of Nyssa, bemoaned the ubiquity of theological debate:

> Every place in the city is full of them: the alleys, the crossroads, the forums, the squares. Garment sellers, money changers, food vendors—they are all at it. If you ask for change, they philosophize for you about generate and ingenerate natures. If you inquire about the price of bread, the answer is that the Father is greater and the Son inferior. If you speak about whether the bath is ready, they express the opinion that the Son was made out of nothing.[12]

Eventually, the debate was settled in the Nicene Creed, and in subsequent creedal statements, in no small part due to the fierce commitment of an Alexandrian deacon named Athanasius. Nicene orthodoxy insisted that the Son was "begotten, not created" and "of one substance of the Father." While these formulations continued to cause controversy, debate, and calls for clarification, the fundamental parameters of Christian orthodoxy have assumed the pre-existence of the Son/ Word/Second Person of the Trinity.

This might all seem like arcane speculation in hindsight, but what it makes clear is the centrality of pre-existence in Christian faith—in the way Christians throughout the centuries have made meaning of the word in light of Jesus Christ. None of these matters are actually settled; debates and tensions and conversations continue. Certain traditions within Protestant Christianity, including my own denomination of the Christian Church (Disciples of Christ), are self-described

---

11. William C. Placher, *A History of Christian Theology: An Introduction* (Louisville: Westminster John Knox, 1983), 73.

12. Cited in Placher, *A History of Christian Theology*, 68.

as non-creedal, and challenge the idea that Christian belief can be codified in credal statements at all. But when the concept of the pre-existence of Christ was enshrined in creeds, the Church Fathers— themselves, of course, wrapped up in a patriarchal worldview and influenced by imperial power—made a statement about what is and isn't pre-existing. To be pre-existent, they reasoned, was to be divine. This was the reason for the passionate debate:

> The assertion that the Word or Son was no more than a creature, no matter how high a creature, provoked angry reactions from many of the bishops: "You lie!" "Blasphemy!" "Heresy!" Eusebius [a proponent of Arius' views] was shouted down, and we are told that his speech was snatched from his hand, torn to shreds, and trampled underfoot.[13]

It makes contemporary church debates seem a bit tame by comparison, no? For Athanasius in particular, the saving work of Christ in history was at stake, an undermining of his irrefutable belief that in Jesus Christ, the very God of the universe had taken up incarnate dwelling among humanity:

> Clearly, the presence of God in history was the central element in the faith of Athanasius. Therefore, it is not surprising that he saw Arianism as a grave threat to the very heart of Christianity. What Arius taught was that the one who had come to us in Jesus Christ was not truly God, but a lesser being, a creature. Such a notion was unacceptable to Athanasius—as it was also to the monks who had withdrawn to the desert for love of God Incarnate, and to the faithful who gathered to participate in worship under Athanasius' leadership. For Athanasius, for the monks, and for many of the faithful, the Arian controversy was not a matter of theological subtleties with little or no relevance. In it, the very core of the Christian message was at stake.[14]

To the contemporary reader, such doctrinal debates may seem out of touch, the equivalent of asking how many angels can dance on a

---

13. González, *Story of Christianity*, 164.

14. González, *Story of Christianity*, 175.

pinhead. But for the early Church, these questions were important because the question of what pre-existed, what came before, was a question about primacy, divinity, and ultimate concern. Naming what came before meant naming God as the source and origin of all reality—prior to imperial power, prior to the collusion of political and religious forces that had executed Jesus, prior to a world of injustice and hurt. Pre-existence mattered.

It mattered, too, because the biblical narratives—first the Hebrew writings (often translated into Greek) that would have been Scripture for the earliest Jesus movement, and later the Greek writings that would come to make up the New Testament—insisted that it mattered. The Scriptures cared about how the story began.

In the Beginning

"In the beginning, God created the heaven and the earth." The King James Version of the opening line of Genesis is certainly one of the most famous "first lines" of English writing, though of course the book of Genesis is not English literature at all. The first, though not the only, creation story in the Jewish and Christian Scriptures arose out of the context of the Ancient Near East. The more recent New Revised Standard Version translation renders the line as, "In the beginning when God created the heavens and the earth." This way of starting the tale tells us something about how the rest of the narrative is going to go. "In the beginning, God"—the story starts with God. There's no explanation for God, no violent origin story for how God became God, a characteristic which differentiates this particular Ancient Near Eastern creation story from many of its contemporaries. God just *is*, and God *is creating*; that's how this story starts. As the story will soon make clear, humans will indeed play a big role, but the story starts with God, and it's God and God's activity that sets the stage for all that is to come. In fact, in this first account of creation in the book of Genesis, while humans are declared to be "very good," it is the Sabbath, God's day of rest, that is the crown of creation, not humanity. The story, even when it is being told by and to humans, begins and ends with God.

For the ancient rabbis, even the Hebrew lettering with which the Genesis text begins points to the reality that God's pre-existence is the starting point for the story:

> The first letter of the first word in the Torah, *'b'reishit*, is the Hebrew letter *bet* [ב]. This prompted the Midrash to suggest that, just as the letter *bet* is enclosed on three sides but open to the front, we are not to speculate on the origins of God or what may have existed before Creation (Gen. R. 1:10). The purpose of such a comment is not to limit the scientific inquiry into the origins of the universe but to discourage efforts to prove the unprovable. It urges us to ask ourselves, "How are we to live in this world?" And it urges us to live facing forward rather than looking backward. Jewish theology generally has been concerned with discerning the will of God rather than proving the existence or probing the nature of God. Ultimate origins ("Who made God?") are hidden from view, but all the rest of the world is open to inquiry. The Torah begins with *bet*, second letter of the Hebrew alphabet, to summon us to begin even if we cannot begin at the very beginning.[15]

The story begins with God, which in turn gives us a place to begin. We seek the presence of God in the midst of our own stories with the faith that God's story precedes, encompasses, and transcends our own.

The story also begins with divine declarations of goodness. While the Western Christian tradition has, in many ways, been dominated by a focus on "original sin," when we start at the beginning of the story we find, instead, a narrative of original goodness, original blessing.[16] God looks over all the things that God created, "and indeed, it was very good" (Genesis 1:31). This core reality of God's goodness, and the goodness of God's creation, with humanity made in this good image,

---

15. *Etz Hayim: Torah and Commentary*, The Rabbinical Assembly—the United Synagogue of Conservative Judaism, ed. David L. Lieber et al. (New York: The Jewish Publication Society, 2001), 3.

16. See Danielle Shroyer, *Original Blessing: Putting Sin in Its Rightful Place* (Fortress Press, 2016), and Matthew Fox, *Original Blessing: A Primer in Creation Spirituality* (TarcherPerigree, 2000).

pre-exists the story of the man and the woman in the garden of Genesis 3, a story which itself does not mention the word "sin" and seems to be an account of humanity's sense of shame and alienation from this basic goodness.[17] Goodness comes first, or, to put it another way, grace comes first. Diana Butler Bass writes of the way that a "gifts-first" approach to the world challenges the benefactor-beneficiary notion of gratitude that dominated Roman imperial society and has continued to affect our contemporary understandings of gratitude:

> There is, however, an alternative structure of gratefulness, one that holds out the possibility of spiritual and ethical transformation—that of *gift and response*. In this mode, gifts exist before benefactors. The universe is a gift. Life is a gift. Air, light, soil, and water are gifts. Friendship, love, sex, and family are gifts. We live on a gifted planet. Everything we need is here, with us. We freely respond to these gifts by choosing a life of mutual care. Some people think of God as the giver of all gifts; others consider these gifts part of nature. Whether you believe God or not-God, however, *gifts come first*.[18]

She points out the connection between the language of gifts, gratitude, and grace:

> The words "gratitude" and "grace" come from the same root word, *gratia* in Latin and *kharis* in Greek. . . . Grace means "unmerited favor." When I think of grace, I particularly like the image of God tossing gifts around—a sort of indiscriminate giver of sustenance, joy, love, and pleasure. Grace—gifts given without being earned and with no expectation of return—is, as the old hymn says, amazing.[19]

In this understanding, gifts, and thus grace, come first, serving as the true original state of being and preceding the "original sin" that has come to dominate much of Western theological thinking.

---

17. See David Finnegan-Hosey, *Christ on the Psych Ward* (New York: Church Publishing, 2018), 44–57.

18. Diana Butler Bass, *Grateful: The Transformative Power of Giving Thanks* (New York: HarperOne, 2018), xxiv. Emphasis mine.

19. Butler Bass, *Grateful*, 19.

To begin with grace and goodness is an important corrective. Without it, the theology of original sin tends to operate as a kind of theological version of diagnostic overshadowing—a term for the tendency of medical professionals to attribute any and all symptoms to a certain disability or chronic condition, such as a mental illness or intellectual disability, thus misdiagnosing or undertreating a patient's pain or illness.[20] By beginning with an implicit assumption of a sort of inherent pathology, rather than an assumption of health or wholeness, doctors can miss or ignore important indicators of detriments to health. The implicit bias behind diagnostic overshadowing is that those with chronic illnesses or intellectual disabilities cannot really be trusted to accurately perceive their own pain or needs.

During the conversational section of a talk I was giving, one young person who had been quiet for most of the session spoke up, "The worst part for me about being diagnosed with a mental illness isn't just that people don't trust me, it's that I'm being told that I can't really trust myself." I share this hurt. The fact that my brain can lie to me sometimes means that there is always the possibility that I am, in fact, inaccurately perceiving my own self. But to have that self-doubt reflected back to me by a medical professional who seems to believe, whether implicitly or explicitly, that they know my experience better than I do is always frustrating. Beyond frustrating, when it leads to misdiagnosis or undertreatment, it can be harmful or even deadly.

Artist and theologian Mary Button speaks about her experiences of diagnostic overshadowing: "It's a type of violence that's perpetrated by the medical community. And once you have a mental health diagnosis then any symptom you have . . . I had a doctor tell me that the strep throat I had was in my head. So everything then becomes a byproduct of your mental illness, and it becomes very difficult to access medical care."[21]

---

20. I owe this insight to a conversation I had at the 2018 Summer Institute for Theology and Disability in Raleigh, NC, with Catherine Webb, M.S. CCC-SLP, a PhD Candidate in Disability Studies at the University of Illinois at Chicago.

21. Mary Button, interview by Marthame Sanders, "Mental Health, Theology, and Creativity—David Finnegan-Hosey & Mary Button" *Wild Goose Festival*, July 14, 2018, available online: *www.youtube.com/watch?v=eJ20wEwKAUs or http://wild goosefestival.org/experience/.*

Diagnostic overshadowing is remarkably similar in its assumptions to the much more conscious desire of insurance companies not to cover those with pre-existing medical conditions: when we start our understanding of someone's health with their pathology or sickness, by viewing them as in some sense untrustworthy or risky, that starting point is likely to dominate and limit our provision of care. This, in addition to their profit motive, is why insurance companies would deny me *any* form of coverage, even basic healthcare, due to my mental illness.

In similar fashion, if we begin our theological story with pathology or sin, this assumption of corruption can overshadow the original goodness with which God creates the cosmos and humanity in God's own image. All sorts of abuse and harm can then be covered over by blanket statements. "All humans are sinful," so this particular instance of harm or un-health can simply be dismissed. "Creation is fallen," so nothing can be done to address unjust or unhealthy systems. To begin with pathology rather than wholeness is to start the story in the wrong place. Where we begin the story matters.

The New Testament stories of Jesus's life take up the Hebrew Bible's interest in beginnings. Just like Genesis, Mark's Gospel starts at the very beginning—literally with the word *beginning*: "The beginning of the good news (or gospel) of Jesus Christ, the Son of God." And then we get a quotation from the prophet Isaiah, and John the Baptizer doing what baptizers do down at the Jordan River. No nativity stories for Mark. No angels or shepherds or magi. No exposition. We just jump right in. His direct, plunge-right-in approach characterizes the rest of Mark's narrative. Mark's Jesus doesn't spend a whole lot of time teaching or dialoguing. He's more of an action-adventure Jesus. One of Mark's favorite words is the Greek *euthys*, often translated as "immediately." The word appears more than forty times in Mark's Gospel, at least six times in the first chapter alone. Jesus seems to do just about everything "immediately." Mark's Gospel doesn't have time to wait around for exposition; it's got stuff to do.

Matthew's Gospel, written after Mark, adds an opening genealogy to show Jesus's lineage and tells stories around Jesus's birth. Luke adds even more prologue, including a John the Baptist origin story, and also expands the genealogy to trace Jesus's line back, not to Abraham as in Matthew, but all the way to Adam and to God's initial creative act. And the Gospel of John, likely the latest written of the four Gospels, famously begins, "In the beginning was the Word, and the Word was with God, and the Word was God. . . . And the Word became flesh and lived among us" (John 1:1, 14).

Whatever sense we make theologically of these words, it's clear that the Gospel writers are interested in beginnings and that, as time goes on, there is an increasingly intensive effort to show that Jesus is part of something that came before—a pre-existent reality. John's account is the pinnacle of this effort.

> For the Gospel of John, the beginning is not a particular event in time like Jesus' birth (as in Matthew and Luke) or the start of Jesus' ministry (as in Mark). Instead, the beginning is outside the normal calculations of time, in the cosmic preexistence of the Word with God. This beginning focuses the reader's attention immediately on the meaning of what follows—the Gospel story is about the very character of God and how God makes Godself known to the world through the life and death of Jesus.[22]

The Word, which in Jesus takes on flesh and lives among us, pre-exists creation with God. The development of Christian belief in this pre-existent Christ begins to differentiate the early Christian communities from the Jewish communities out of which they originated, so that in a very real way, to be Christian means to believe something different about what pre-exists and what doesn't.[23] And yet this differentiation of belief contains within it a resonance of belief: what pre-exists is divine, is good, is gift. Grace, not sin or pathology or brokenness, is the true pre-existing condition of creation.

---

22. Gail R. O'Day, commentary on "The Gospel According to John," in *The New Interpreter's Study Bible: New Revised Standard Version with the Apocrypha* (Nashville: Abingdon, 2003), 1908.

23. While I am speaking here of the differentiation in terms of belief and practice, it is important to name the reality that much Christian differentiation from its Jewish roots took on supremacist and violent forms, from supercessionism to attacks on the Jewish community. This violence continues to echo in contemporary anti-Semitism and white nationalism, and must be repudiated.

The Case for Grace

If the stories of Jesus show an increasing concern for matters of beginnings, the letter to the Ephesians puts this concern with pre-existence explicitly in the context of a theology of grace. The "mystery of God's will," according to the author of Ephesians, is God's "plan for the fullness of time," the original divine desire to "gather up all things in Christ, things in heaven and things on earth" (Ephesians 1:10). God's plan for all of time is reflected in what humanity is created for and saved for: "For we are what God has made us, created in Christ Jesus [note the shared theology here with John's Gospel, in which creation occurs in and through Christ] for good works, which God prepared beforehand to be our way of life" (Ephesians 2:10). Creation and salvation, by grace, are the pre-condition established by God, for humanity's work for the common good. Recall the connection made by Diana Butler Bass between grace, gratitude, and gift. Grace, the unmerited gifting of all creation, is not an ex post facto divine intervention to try to fix humanity's brokenness; rather, it is the pre-existing condition of all creation. We are declared "good" before we are declared anything else—an essential wholeness of humanity created in the image of God versus the brokenness of our human-made systems.

There is, then, a deeper truth underlying my visceral reaction to the term "pre-existing condition" in its medical sense. To begin the story with pathology or illness is to start in the wrong place, a form of heresy. Not surprisingly, starting the story there, rather than with an original condition of graciously created wholeness, inevitably leads to limits on the provision of care. Rather than a holistic view of humanity, created in original goodness and sharing in the contingencies and dependencies of all of creation, we end up with a divided view of "sick" humans and "well" humans. In turn, we end up with a system that focuses on divining who is risky and who isn't, rather than on providing care for all—a system that is actually built for those least in need of it.

2

Insurance and Assurance

In the United States, insurance—and thus the healthcare that it allows access to—is for the healthy, not the sick. The system is built for those least in need of it. This is certainly true if protections for pre-existing conditions don't exist. If insurers can deny coverage based on someone's previous illness, then once you get sick, it's harder to get healthcare in the future. But the statement is also true more broadly.

The sicker someone is, the more difficult it is to navigate the already confusing world of health insurance. Some of the most taxing experiences I've had in terms of my mental health have come, not while in a hospital psychiatric unit, but sitting at home on the phone with this or that insurance provider. These experiences come with the normal stresses of remote customer service—long wait times, representatives with little power or understanding of my mental health or coverage needs, being bounced from one department to another as if the insurance company is a giant pinball machine—in addition to the added stress of trying to navigate the system with a mental illness. Anxiety, depression, and mood dysregulation add layers of challenge to the process. What's more, the inherent flaw of health insurance being for the healthy is baked into the system, because insurance, at its core, is about risk management. Within that calculus, sick people are riskier than healthy people.

Of course, the idea that health insurance is for healthy people, not sick people, assumes some sort of dichotomy between "healthy" and "sick," which we all know, if we are being honest with ourselves, is simply not true. Everybody gets sick sometimes. So it is probably not surprising that a system built for the healthiest people actually fails to protect millions of people. In 2013, prior to the implementation of key provisions of the Affordable Care Act including protections for pre-existing conditions, around 44 million people in the United States did not have insurance coverage; by 2017, that number had fallen to 27.4 million, though that figure still represents close to 9 percent of the U.S. population.[1] And almost half of U.S. Americans rely on their employer for health insurance, meaning that the loss of a job, possibly due to a medical condition, would lead to a loss in their coverage.[2] These numbers represent more than just an economic reality for many in the United States. A 2009 study conducted by the Harvard Medical School and the Cambridge Health Alliance, for example, found that nearly 45 thousand deaths a year could be linked to a lack of healthcare coverage, more deaths annually than widespread conditions like kidney disease.[3] A more recent survey of similar studies confirmed this link between lack of health insurance coverage and higher mortality rates.[4] For many in this country, lack of insurance is fatal.

None of this is particularly surprising in a for-profit insurance system. According to *Axios*, "Aetna, Anthem, Cigna, Humana and UnitedHealth Group—the big five for-profit insurers—cumulatively collected $4.5 billion in net earnings in the first three months of 2017."[5]

---

1. Kaiser Family Foundation, "Key Facts about the Uninsured Population," published December 7, 2018, available online at: *https://www.kff.org/uninsured/fact-sheet/key-facts-about-the-uninsured-population/*.

2. Kaiser Family Foundation, "Health Insurance Coverage of the Total Population," searchable database available online at *https://www.kff.org/other/state-indicator/total-population*.

3. David Cecare, "New study finds 45,000 deaths annually linked to lack of health coverage," *The Harvard Gazette*, September 17, 2009, available online: *https://news.harvard.edu/gazette/story/2009/09/new-study-finds-45000-deaths-annually-linked-to-lack-of-health-coverage/*.

4. S. Woolhandler and D. U. Himmelstein, "The Relationship of Health Insurance and Mortality: Is Lack of Insurance Deadly?," *Annals of Internal Medicine*, September 19, 2017, available online: *https://annals.org/aim/fullarticle/2635326/relationship-health-insurance-mortality-lack-insurance-deadly*.

5. Bob Herman, "Profits are booming at health insurance companies," *Axios*, May 24, 2017, available online: *www.axios.com/profits-are-booming-at-health-insurance-companies-1513302495-18f3710a-c0b4-4ce3-8b7f-894a755e6679.html*.

In 2018, David Wichmann, the CEO of UnitedHealth Group, had a total compensation of $21.5 million, including a $1.3 million annual salary, $5.4 million in incentive pay, and $14.5 million in shares, all of which adds up to 316 times more than the $57,412 salary of the average UnitedHealth employee.[6] To make this kind of profit, insurance companies have to gamble that the people they insure will remain healthy, which disincentivizes covering those who are sick. The more expensive the sickness, the more intense the disincentive. The gamble pays off only if people don't have to access the care that the coverage is supposed to insure. The insurance company makes the gamble; the consumer, meanwhile, makes a gamble of their own to buy coverage, if they can afford it, based on the future risk of sickness. This is why insurance companies, in the absence of legal prohibitions against it, would prefer to be able to deny coverage to those with a pre-existing condition: it stacks the deck in their favor.

We buy insurance because we think the risk of a future illness or calamity is greater than the immediate cost of the purchase. Much modern Christian theology has adopted this risk management approach to a core component of faith: salvation. The infamous, though often misinterpreted, logic of Pascal's Wager pops up in a variety of forms throughout popular Christianity, urging hypothetical nonbelievers to take the safe bet on eternity by believing.[7] Tongue-in-cheek church signs urge passersby to come inside for "fire insurance," a rather apt metaphor for much of American Christianity, which views accepting Jesus as a personal savior as a get-out-of-Hell-free card. Salvation, in this view, is about risk management. It's insurance. One buys in, the price of admission perhaps being a confession of sin, a dunk in a baptismal pool, or the praying of a set prayer, in order to avoid the future risk of hell.

---

6. Morgan Haefner, "UnitedHealth CEO's 2018 compensation: $21.5M," *Becker's Hospital Review*, April 23, 2019, available online: *https://www.beckershospitalreview. com/payer-issues/unitedhealth-ceo-s-2018-compensation-21-5m.html.*

7. French theologian and philosopher Blaise Pascal's "'Wager,'" part of a posthumously published work called *Pensees*, was actually a piece of a longer argument against the use of logical proofs for the existence of God as a way to convince people to believe—in other words, an argument against precisely the kind of logic with which the Wager is often employed.

Insurance vs. Assurance

The parallel between this schema of salvation and the risk management motivation that impacts far too much of the U.S. healthcare system strikes me as an impoverished view of salvation. In fact, there is a theological concept that stands in tension to this risk management approach to salvation: not insurance, but rather, assurance. Christian thinkers have differed on the question of whether a person can truly be assured of their salvation. Justo L. González defines assurance as the "complete and absolute knowledge of one's salvation" and notes that "[w]hether or not this is possible has been much debated, particularly since the time of the Reformation," with the Catholic position tending to be that the experience of assurance only came to a select group of believers, while the Lutheran and Calvinist position was to ground assurance, not in human experience, but in the objective truth of the gospel message.[8] In their 1999 *Joint Declaration on the Doctrine of Justification,* the Lutheran World Federation and the Roman Catholic Church attempted to arrive at a shared understanding of these Reformation-era debates, stating "We confess together that the faithful can rely on the mercy and promises of God. In spite of their own weakness and the manifold threats to their faith, on the strength of Christ's death and resurrection they can build on the effective promise of God's grace in Word and Sacrament and so be sure of this grace."[9]

The Anglican priest John Wesley, one of the founders of the eighteenth-century Methodist movement (the tradition in which I received much of my faith formation), held strongly to a view of assurance of salvation as a gift of the Holy Spirit that could actually be experienced by the person of faith. Wesley described his own experience of this assurance as the sensation of having his "heart strangely warmed" at a Moravian gathering on Aldersgate Street in London, after which he wrote in his journal, "I felt I did trust in

---

8. Justo L. González, *Essential Theological Terms* (Louisville: Westminster John Knox, 2005), 20.

9. *Joint Declaration on the Doctrine of Justification*, The Lutheran World Federation and The Roman Catholic Church—Pontifical Council for Promoting Christian Unity, English-language Edition (Grand Rapids, MI: William B. Eerdmans, 2000), 23.

Christ, Christ alone for salvation; and an assurance was given me that He had taken away my sins, even mine, and saved me from the law of sin and death;" the moment is still celebrated by modern-day Methodists as "Aldersgate Day."[10]

In a sermon entitled "The Witness of the Spirit," Wesley defended his understanding of assurance in reference to Romans 8, saying, "If we are wise we shall be continually crying to God, until his Spirit cry in our heart, 'Abba, Father!' This is the privilege of all the children of God, and *without this we can never be assured that we are his children*."[11] Notably, in responding to critiques of his doctrine of assurance, Wesley cites his theological opponents' claim that such an experience of assurance may simply be a side effect of mental illness, putting the following objection into the mouths of his interlocuters: "But madmen, French prophets, and enthusiasts of every kind have imagined they experienced this witness."[12] Apparently, Wesley's rivals were quite concerned that those of us with mental illness would stumble into a delusion of our own salvation! The tradition I now identify with, the Christian Church (Disciples of Christ), also has a historic emphasis on assurance of salvation. Alexander Campbell was one of the founders of the movement that would become the modern-day Disciples of Christ. His writings on salvation emphasized "the assurance and enjoyment of forgiveness," a focus that "is understandable given Campbell's engagement with the [American] frontier's search for the assurance of forgiveness."[13] Against backgrounds of uncertainty and anxiety, reformers and revivalists like Wesley and Campbell emphasized that believers could have sure knowledge of God's grace in their lives, a message that was received

---

10. United Methodist Church Discipleship Ministries, "What is Aldersgate Day?," available online at *http://www.umc.org/what-we-believe/what-is-aldersgate-day*.

11. John Wesley, "The Witness of the Spirit—Discourse II," in *John Wesley's Sermons: An Anthology*, ed. Albert C. Outler and Richard P. Heitzenrater (Nashville: Abingdon, 1991), 402. Emphasis added.

12. Ibid., 399.

13. John Mark Hicks, "Salvation," in *The Encyclopedia of the Stone-Campbell Movement*, ed. Douglas A. Foster, Paul M. Blowers, Anthony L. Dunnavant, and D. Newell Williams (Grand Rapids, MI: William B. Eerdmans, 2004), 664.

as good news by people whose lives granted them little sense of stability or safety.[14] Not surprisingly, given my Methodist roots and current ministry within a Disciples of Christ context, assurance is an important component of my own faith journey.

In 2005, during my sophomore year of college, I studied abroad in Morocco. I had nearly mystical expectations built up in my head about the life-changing experience I was going to have there; and yet I found myself unexpectedly homesick, reeling from culture shock, and struggling to relate to people in healthy ways. Looking back at that time, I can see I often acted out of a sense of entitlement that was against my core values and against the reasons I wanted to study abroad to begin with. While I was far away from home, my dad was admitted into the hospital with his own mental health struggles. I was having a hard time.

I became part of a small Christian community that met in an apartment just off campus. As you might imagine, there weren't a lot of church options available in Morocco, and so we all met together in one community, despite our different backgrounds: Roman Catholic, Armenian Orthodox, Methodist, Pentecostal, and Baptist. Our pastor, the Rev. Karen Thomas Smith, who also served as the interfaith chaplain for the university, was ordained by the Alliance of Baptists. She was incredibly gifted at facilitating community among such a diverse group of people—both our very different Christian backgrounds and with our Muslim classmates, colleagues, and neighbors. I had grown up in church and had always viewed church as something of an extended family. But it was this small community in Morocco where I truly fell in love with a vision of what church could be.

During one of our Sunday evening worship gatherings, Karen delivered a message based on a Scripture reading from Matthew's Gospel. To be honest, I've forgotten the topic of the sermon, but I do remember one thing clearly. She began by talking about the Gospel

---

14. It's important to note that the term "American Frontier" is not value neutral, and in fact erases the experience of those people for whom the land was not a frontier but their ancient ancestral homes. The emphasis on individual assurance can have a shadow side, ignoring the broader impacts of forces such as colonialism.

as a whole, and about how thinking where the passage sat in the longer narrative was key to understanding it. She challenged us to read
through all of Matthew that week, and to read it as a story, looking for
all of the elements that make for a good story: character development,
narrative tension, dramatic irony, foreshadowing, climax.

I had not thought of that before. I went home and read through
the whole gospel that night. And when I read the last words ("And
remember, I am with you always, to the end of the age."), I remember
setting my Bible down and saying, out loud, in a hushed tone so as not
to wake my roommate, "Oh, I get it. It's a story."

I don't mean that I realized it was a work of fiction; rather that it
was a full narrative, not a collection of disconnected rules and unreal-
istic moral demands. It was a story, with rhythms and dynamics and
growth and change, and what's more, it was a story into which I was
invited. It included me.

"Remember I am with you always," the story ended. As I set down
the book I could sense a shift, the settling down of the anxious ques-
tioning, much of it driven by a secret self-loathing that was swirling
about in my head. In its place, a sense of assurance sank down into my
heart. This story included me. Jesus had promised to be with me. God
loved me; yes, even me.

This is not to say that my experience of assurance has led me to
some sort of unassailable certainty. I don't understand assurance as a
cure-all for doubt or hurt, an interpretation that I fear some strands
of post-Reformation Christian theology do indeed fall into. And as
someone with a mental illness, I am acutely aware of the danger of
basing faith entirely on the subjectivity of one's own feelings or emotions. Sometimes, my feelings try to kill me; to someone suffering
from depression or anxiety, the "feeling" of assurance may seem simply out of reach. This, to me, is what is so vital about the sufficiency
or "enough-ness" of grace.[15] Assurance is not a matter of constant and
objective certainty. It is the conviction that one is truly included in

---

15. David Finnegan-Hosey, *Christ on the Psych Ward* (New York: Church Publishing,
2018), 59–75.

the story of God's sufficient grace. It is more than a trite statement like, "Everything's going to be fine." Perhaps the fourteenth-century mystic, Julian of Norwich, captured it more closely: "All shall be well, and all shall be well, and all manner of things shall be well." Assurance says, "You—yes you—you are part of this tale. And you will have enough. Enough for wellness. Enough for wholeness. Enough for life."

Assurance of Healing

This assurance-based approach to salvation is healthier than a view of salvation as insurance against the risk of fiery damnation. And there is a further layer to this distinction, which returns us to where we began—the conversation around the U.S. healthcare system and the provision of care to those in need. It has to do with the word "salvation" itself, the very reality of which we can be assured. The English word "salvation" is, as is the case with many theological terms, a translation, in this case from the Greek of the New Testament. The Greek root, *sozo*, can be translated "save," but also "heal" or "make whole," a connection in meaning that can also be heard in the English words "save" and "salve." One can be saved from death or sickness, and a wound can be salved to assist in its healing.

Western Christianity has tended to entirely spiritualize salvation, making it something that has to do with life after death and not with an embodied reality in the present. But this dichotomy is foreign to the world of the Scriptures. The biblical origins of the term are holistic, encompassing both spiritual and bodily realities. Jesus's name in Aramaic, Yeshua, is from the Hebrew for "God saves," which would have included the meaning of concrete liberation from oppression. And Jesus's ministry is an incarnational embodiment of exactly this holistic sense of liberation and salvation. For example, in Matthew's Gospel, a woman attempts to touch the fringe of Jesus's cloak, saying, "If I only touch his cloak, I will be made well" (Matthew 9:21). Jesus responds, saying, "Take heart, daughter; your faith has made you well" (Matthew 9:22). Both instances of "made well" have the root *sozo*: your faith has "saved you," has "made you well." Assurance of salvation—a sense of being included in the story, of having enough for health and life—takes on immediate concrete meaning when we realize the word salvation is itself deeply related to healing. If assurance of salvation is assurance of healing, assurance of wholeness, then it offers a different perspective than an insurance system based on health risk management. When we bring this theological language to the discussion of healthcare, we reveal the gaps between our current system and a view of the world as divinely created, essentially good, and intended for human flourishing—life abundant.

I want to pause here to acknowledge that narratives around health and wholeness can actually create barriers to the holistic experiences of people with chronic illnesses and disability, including mental illness. When I speak of "wholeness," I am speaking of a God who sees our wholeness when the world sees brokenness or fragmentation. Often, people with disabilities and chronic illnesses receive a message that they are, in and of themselves, broken, and that they must dedicate their lives to being healthy and whole—often by trying whatever homegrown cure, diet, or out-of-the-mainstream treatment happened to work for their interlocuter (or even worse, the nephew of their interlocuter). Hailey Joy Scandrette writes of this in relation to her own experience of chronic illness in a blog post entitled "Treatment Burnout":

> There is so much pressure as someone with a chronic illness to work towards "getting better." . . . I am allowed to wish I wasn't sick, I am allowed to be angry about being sick, but I am also allowed to accept that I am sick, and that physical health is not my purpose in life. . . . As this year ends, I am working to imagine a future for myself where I feel like a full person without health as a prerequisite. This is challenging when I feel constantly bombarded with cultural messaging that declares that physical health is not only imperative to happiness and success, but also a marker of moral character, beauty, and worth. On some level it seems innocuous to encourage people to prioritize health, but when I buy into that narrative I lose so much of myself. I am learning that

it doesn't improve my life to prioritize my physical health over my emotional health, my sense of self, my passions, or my connection with other human beings.[16]

Whatever healing is, it must both be an embodied reality and include those for whom physical healing might not look like what societal expectations assume it will, which raises an important question: if salvation is related to healing and wholeness, is it available to all, or only for a select few?

Individual and Universal on the Debate Stage

During the first round of the 2019 Democratic Primary Debates, moderator Lester Holt of NBC posed a question to the twenty candidates: "Who here would abolish their private health insurance in favor of a government-run plan?" While several would later claim that they had misunderstood the question, it nevertheless revealed significant differences in perspective in a primary otherwise marked by a relative consensus on the key issues.[17]

Underlying Holt's question and the varied responses is a basic question about healthcare in the United States. Is healthcare a universal right, and thus one that a state (at least a democratic one) has a basic obligation to provide, or is healthcare a private matter and, by extension, is its availability determined by the ability of an individual or family to afford it? The significant complexities of the question and the policy debates surrounding it call for more than this binary choice. Nevertheless, as I listened to the debate, and as the Trump administration continued to support efforts in federal courts to abolish the Affordable Care Act, I couldn't shake a sense of familiarity. I had heard this debate before, but in a different context.

---

16. Hailey Joy Scandrette, "Treatment Burnout," December 20, 2018, available online: *https://haileyjs.wordpress.com/2018/12/20/treatment-burnout/*.

17. Dan Merica, "Kamala Harris says she misinterpreted question on abolishing private insurance," *CNN*, June 28, 2019, available online: *https://www.cnn.com/2019/06/28/politics/kamala-harris-democratic-debate-abolishing-private-insurance/index.html*.

In my seminary classes, we had similar discussions about the distinction between a private system accessible to an elect few, the meaning and quality of which is determined in part by its selectivity, and a universal system intended for all. Only we weren't talking about healthcare. We were talking about salvation.

Christian theological understandings of salvation, including different understandings of who is included in God's gracious saving work, are myriad. In the strict Calvinist understanding, atonement is limited, and salvation is intended only for an elect few, chosen even before time began. This understanding is intended to protect the sovereignty of God and to eliminate any hint of human participation in salvation. God alone makes the choice of who is saved and who is not. A different theological position, known as Arminianism after the Dutch theologian Jacobus Arminius (himself, it's worth noting, from a Calvinist background), rejects this strict Calvinist understanding in favor of human free will. While humans still do not "earn" their salvation through their works, they do have the choice to participate in God's saving work, though that choice is itself only available to them as a gift of grace. Modern-day Methodists, among others, are inheritors of the Arminian tradition. John Wesley, one of the founders of the Methodist movement, insisted that humans were saved by grace alone while also emphasizing the importance of participation in the "means of grace," such as communion, and acknowledging that humans, through their own free will, could resist or reject God's grace.

Yet another, sometimes intertwining, position is known as universalism: the simple idea that all people are saved. Critics of this perspective have often pointed out that, like strict Calvinism, this account of salvation denies any human free will. If all are saved, can humans say "no" to God? For some universalists, an argument for free will that includes the freedom to suffer in horrific eternal punishment does not seem particularly concerned with a robust account of what "freedom" means at all. Some who hold the universalist position, however, argue instead that universal salvation is not contrary to free will; instead, humans will eventually be won over by God's love by their own volition, an understanding which has been succinctly described as "Love wins."[18] Similarly, process theologians argue that, while God cannot force humans into anything, God never gives up in drawing people toward goodness by way of God's non-coercive love.

All of these understandings may seem theoretical, but they take on a more immediate meaning if we remember the connection between salvation and healing, wholeness, and liberation. Is healing, and by extension the systems of care that allow for health, for a select few? Is it for everyone? If it's for everyone, does forcing people to have a particular form of care constitute a violation of their freedoms?

As I write this, these different understandings are playing out in overt ways in the lead-up to the 2020 presidential election. Conservative political forces, including the current administration, argue that the Affordable Care Act, by making people either buy insurance or pay a financial penalty, violates their individual freedom, which must take precedence over any sort of guaranteed access to healthcare. More progressive political movements argue that healthcare for all needs to have priority but disagree on how to reach this goal. The Medicare for All plan supported by politicians such as Bernie Sanders and Elizabeth Warren, for example, would eventually eliminate private insurance, at least in its present form (some would argue that some supplemental forms of private insurance could still exist).[19] Other plans, such as Medicare for America, call for an optional buy-in to government-funded plans, with private insurance as a continuing option.[20]

---

18. See Rob Bell, *Love Wins: A Book About Heaven, Hell, and the Fate of Every Person Who Has Ever Lived* (New York: HarperOne, 2011).

19. It is also worth noting that many disability rights activists worry that Medicare for All leaves out the important provisions within Medicaid that allow people with disabilities to live in the community rather than being homebound or living in institutional settings. See Robyn Powell, "'Medicare for All' Must Truly Be for All—Including People with Disabilities," *Rewire.News*, March 13, 2019, available online: *https://rewire.news/article/2019/03/13/medicare-for-all-must-truly-be-for-all-including-people-with-disabilities/*.

20. Dylan Scott, "Medicare for America, Beto O'Rourke's Favorite Healthcare Plan, Explained," *Vox*, March 18, 2019, available online: *https://www.vox.com/policy-and-politics/2019/3/18/18270857/medicare-for-all-beto-orourke-2020-policies-voxcare*.

Some proponents of this latter plan make an argument similar to that made by some universalists: while we should not force anyone into having a universal healthcare system, given the option people will choose it of their own free will. In other words, people will have a choice, but given the true choice, they will eventually choose a universal system. Again, our conversation about healthcare in this country is remarkably, even if unintentionally, theological.

What I've Come to Believe

I confess to personally being somewhat agnostic as to the absolute best policy framework for healthcare in the United States, or at least a pragmatist. What I want is the solution that gives everybody good healthcare, myself included, with protections for those like me with pre-existing conditions and equal treatment of mental health along with physical health. I suspect that there are multiple policy frameworks that could potentially achieve that goal. While my formation in the Methodist tradition made me particularly sympathetic to Arminian theology, and my engagement in ecumenical and interfaith ministry (not to mention campus ministry, which necessitates a healthy amount of conversation with those who do not affiliate with a particular religious tradition and are often skeptical of the whole mess) has tended to lead me toward universalist understandings of salvation, I similarly have no unique insight into the details of how matters of eternity really play out.

In spite of my agnosticism, or perhaps because of it, I have come to believe a few things. If we begin with the assumption that all are included within the horizon of care, we will end up with healthier attitudes, healthier behaviors, and healthier systems. Whatever the initial motivation for belief in a design intended only for a select few, the inevitable end result of such constructions is the privileging of the "elect" at the expense of the marginalized, oppressed, and excluded. Calvin's understanding of salvation may initially have been understood as a pastoral response to anxieties about assurance—how do I know I am saved?—but over time, strict Calvinism has led steadily to a risk-management, insurance-based understanding of salvation, not to mention that particular combination of theology and capitalism known as the Protestant work ethic. In other words, rather than an anxiety-reducing assurance that salvation is in God's hands, belief in salvation for an elect few has created a belief, not always conscious, that the elect can be identified as the privileged in society, those who benefit from the dominant socioeconomic system. "Hard work" (read, those who are able to climb the economic ladder) is indicative of salvation. Rather than God's absolute freedom, human ability to work becomes the measure of salvation—a works-based righteousness.

Similarly, a healthcare system built only for a select few "healthy" people is, in a literal sense, works-based: those with jobs are worthy of healthcare coverage, those without are left without or are stereotyped as drains on the system. Medicaid recipients, who fall under a certain poverty threshold, particularly in states such as where I live in North Carolina that refused to expand Medicaid under the Affordable Care Act, experience stigma and policies targeted against them, in a way that recipients of Medicare, perceived as retired people who have earned their keep, do not. I have come to believe that Christians, whose understanding of healing and wholeness should, at least in theory, be based in an understanding of unearned, unmerited grace, ought to be suspicious of this kind of belief in "earning" access to healthcare, at least as suspicious as we claim to be of the idea of earning one's salvation.

And finally, when it comes to matters of salvation, assurance, and eternity, I have come to believe what a man named Paul wrote in an old, old letter to a new community of faith in a very powerful capital city: "For I am convinced that neither death, nor life, nor angels, nor rulers, nor things present, nor things to come, nor powers, nor height, nor depth, nor anything else in all creation, will be able to separate us from the love of God in Christ Jesus our Lord" (Romans 8:38–39). I don't claim to know with any certainty what Paul's words about the love of God in Christ Jesus mean in terms of the various theological understandings of salvation held by Christians over the centuries. But as I said before, assurance, for me, is not about certainty. "Nothing can separate us from the love of God in Christ Jesus." Not sickness, not pre-existing conditions, not unjust systems designed for the privileged few rather than the many, not even death.

It is these words from which I draw my assurance—not in order to hedge my bets against some future suffering, but as a reminder, in the here and now and always, that I am deeply loved and cared for—and that I can, in turn, be an agent of that love and caring for others. In fact, both the words "assurance" and "insurance" have at their root the Latin word *cura*: care. What would it look like to have a health system truly based in this root of care, for all of us? For in the reality of God's love, we are less separated than we are deeply connected.

3

Forgive Us Our Debts

Recently, I had lunch with a friend whom I had first met while living in that basement apartment in D.C. It had been some time since we had seen each other, so we spent the first half of the meal getting caught up and sharing news about mutual friends. I mentioned that I had just started working on a second book (shameless self-promotion being an inevitable job hazard of the publishing world) and that one of the topics I was going to address was related to medical debt. "Oh, yeah," my friend said, "I have vivid memories of when I first met you. You were so anxious about your debt. It was almost paralyzing for you. I remember how hopeless you felt about the future."

Her words took me back to what I felt in that time: anxiety, fear, and despair stemming from my newly diagnosed mental illness, yes, but also from the crushing weight of the debt from multiple hospitalizations, almost none of which had been covered by insurance. By the time I returned to D.C. from Silver Hill Hospital in Connecticut, I owed almost $80,000. My monthly payments added up to more than my rent, a statement that ought to shock anyone who has ever had to look for housing in our nation's capital. At the time, it was impossible for me to imagine getting out from under the mountain of debt and hard to imagine ever having employment that could make the payments manageable, much less pay off the debt completely. I thought about my debt nearly every minute of every day. It impacted the way I thought about my future, about my education, about my calling. I have no idea how I would have survived that time without economic support from my family, a privilege that is a distant fantasy for many, many people in our country.

I was far from alone in the stress caused by medical debt. It is one of the most widespread financial challenges in the United States.

> [Researchers] found that one in six Americans have past-due healthcare bills on their credit report, a debt totaling $81 billion in all. More than half of these bills—53 percent—amount to less than $600 each. These findings are consistent with a 2017 Urban Institute report that suggested medical debt is the most common financial burden in collections in the United States, a country where healthcare spending amounts to 18 percent of the nation's gross domestic product.[1]

Medical debt disproportionately impacts people who do not have insurance, and particularly clusters around those who have just aged out of access to their parent's insurance plans.[2] The Poor People's Campaign (relaunched fifty years after the assassination of the Rev. Dr. Martin Luther King Jr., who was working on the campaign when he died) has pointed out the link between lack of health insurance, medical debt, and other forms of debt in driving poverty and inequality in the United States:

> There are 32 million people who lack health insurance. Further, an estimated 40 percent of Americans have taken on debt because of medical issues, making medical debt the number one cause of personal bankruptcy filings. In fact, the bottom 90 percent of Americans [in terms of wealth] hold more than 70 percent of debt in the country. Student debt has grown to $1.34 trillion and affects 44 million Americans. Excluding the value of the family car, 19 percent of all U.S. households have zero wealth or negative net worth. They owe more than they own.[3]

---

1. Laura Santhanam, "Millennials rack up the most medical debt, and more frequently," *PBS News Hour*, July 26, 2018, available online: *https://www.pbs.org/newshour/health/millennials-rack-up-the-most-medical-debt-and-more-frequently*.

2. Ibid.

3. Poor People's Campaign, "A Moral Agenda Based on Fundamental Rights," available online: *https://www.poorpeoplescampaign.org/demands/*.

Along with the common nature of medical debt come the additional stresses and mental health challenges associated with it. Debt haunts you. It's difficult, if not impossible, to plan for the future, especially if you are continuing to deal with a long-term or chronic illness which landed you in debt in the first place. Many people avoid medical care, particularly preventive medical care, due to the burden or potential burden of medical debt, which leads to an intensifying spiral of delayed healthcare leading to higher eventual healthcare costs leading to increased anxiety leading to more need for care. Credit scores can be affected for years by debt caused by a medical emergency or needed care. Debt collectors can call and harass people with unpaid bills.

One hospital in particular had the bad habit of sending me a bill with all-caps font telling me I had failed to make a payment when I had, in fact, already made a payment. I would call the hospital in a panic only to hear that, since the hospital contracts out its billing services, there was a lag time between the payment being received by the hospital and the billing company knowing that the bill had been paid. When I expressed frustration with a mental healthcare facility creating added anxiety with this kind of practice, I was met with predictable indifference. The irony was that my biggest mental health challenge was dealing with the mental healthcare system and the debt I had incurred within it.

An Ancient-Modern Prayer for an Ancient-Modern Problem

As the reality of debt began to weigh on me, I was reminded of a lesson from my first year of seminary. I had begun working with a nearby campus ministry, and was given responsibility for the part of the weekly worship service where students shared joys and concerns. I then gathered those prayer requests up in a pastoral prayer, ending in the Lord's Prayer, which, in the form in which we were accustomed to praying it, goes like this:

Our Father,
> who art in Heaven,
> hallowed be thy name.

Thy kingdom come,
> thy will be done,
> on earth as it is in heaven.

Give us this day our daily bread,
> and forgive us our trespasses,
> as we forgive those who trespass against us.

And lead us not into temptation,
> but deliver us from evil;
> for thine is the kingdom, and the power, and the glory forever.

Amen.

The campus ministry was an ecumenical community, made up of students from a variety of religious (and non-religious) backgrounds. One of my students said they were always thrown off by the version of the Lord's Prayer that we used because it was different from the translation they had grown up praying. The version they were used to said, "Forgive us our debts," rather than "Forgive us our trespasses."

"Yes!" I over-emoted. "That's actually an accurate translation." As I started to launch into minister-splaining, a sudden moment of realization washed over me. Everything I was about to share with this student about debt and forgiveness in Scripture were things that were more relevant for me than they had ever been in my life.

The prayer that Jesus taught the disciples appears in two slightly different versions in Scripture, in Matthew's and Luke's Gospels. In both instances, the familiar prayer challenges oversimplified dichotomies between personal and communal spirituality, between public and private faith, and between the breaking-in of God's heavenly realm and the realities of earthly life. As with all of our biblical texts, the Gospels of Matthew and Luke are written in the contexts of communities. Matthew, in particular, is "the only Gospel to use the [Greek term translated as] 'church,' *ekklesia*," and "both its contents and structure indicate an interest in providing clear and coherent guidance to a *community of believers*."[4] The entire Gospel emphasizes a concern with community, portraying the church as an extension of the story of God's people as recounted in the Hebrew Bible and focusing on the reign, or as it is often translated, the kingdom, of God; both "reign" and "kingdom," of course, being political and social terms.

In Matthew's Gospel, Jesus's teaching on prayer at first seems to be in tension with this wider communal emphasis. It occurs within a section of teaching that warns disciples not to practice piety publicly in order to be impressive to others. As such, Matthew's Jesus seems to commend private prayer to the disciples: "Go into your room and shut the door and pray to your Father who is in secret" (Matthew 6:6a).[5] The second person used in this instruction is singular—that is, you, an individual disciple, go into your individual room and pray—which is fascinating given the consistent use of the first person plural in the prayer itself, beginning with that very first word, "Our." Furthermore, the instruction to pray privately—unlike the hypocrites or "play-actors" who "stand and pray in the synagogues and at the street corners so that they may be seen by others" (Matthew 6:5)—seems to be in contradiction to Jesus's earlier instruction to "let your light shine before others, so that they may see your good works and give glory to your Father in heaven" (5:16). Which is it, Jesus? Humble private prayer, or public good works for the glory of God?

A closer look at Matthew 6:5–13 provides insight into how disciples are to live in this creative tension between private piety and public action. The prayer taught by Jesus, even if said in private, is deeply communal. God is addressed communally (that first word, "Our") and the second of three petitions of the prayer is also in the first-person

---

4. Luke Timothy Johnson, *The Writings of the New Testament: An Interpretation* (Minneapolis: Fortress Press, 1999), 187. Emphasis added.

5. Throughout this chapter, I will rely on traditional translations of these passages and thus will be citing masculine images of God. It is vitally important that we employ a range of images for God and that we address the ways in which masculine images have been used to enforce patriarchal understandings and power structures. For more on this topic in relation with mental health, see David Finnegan-Hosey, *Christ on the Psych Ward* (New York: Church Publishing, 2018), 76–91.

plural. Even when praying in private, a disciple prays in community. Furthermore, the prayer taught by Jesus is explicitly a prayer for the coming reign or kingdom of God. The action of God in bringing about the present reality of God has holistic consequences that cannot be understood in individualistic terms.

The prayer taught by Jesus provides a description of the reign of God that is both a future hope and a present, even if hidden, reality. The kingdom is present when God's will is done in present earthly reality just as it will be in a future heavenly realm. The kingdom creates a reality in which all people have their "daily bread," a phrase that can be understood quite literally as a reference to present needs—the things we all need to get through the day—as well as to a future heavenly banquet.[6] Unlike the bread that Jesus is urged to create by the tempter in Matthew 4:3,[7] the daily bread for which the disciples are to pray includes all that is needed for life with God.

All of which brings us back to debts. The word I grew up praying as "trespasses" is the Greek word *opheilēmata*, which literally means "debts." In Luke's Gospel, a different word is initially used, usually translated as "sins," but then Luke reverts back to *opheilonti*, so that the stanza in the New Revised Standard Version translation reads: "Forgive us our *sins*, for we ourselves forgive everyone *indebted* to us" (Luke 11:4). In both cases, minus any other context, the word would mean a material debt owed to someone. This literal meaning is highlighted by the fact that Jesus, in Matthew's Gospel, adds an additional explanation regarding interpersonal forgiveness, an explanation that would presumably be unnecessary if the early hearer or reader of the text would have assumed that the debts being referred to were related to interpersonal behavior rather than monetary exchanges. Similarly, in Matthew 18:23–35, a story about literal debts is employed as a parable to lead to commentary on the need to forgive each other in community. Both passages seem to indicate that Jesus's listeners would have

---

6. Leander E. Keck et al., *The New Interpreter's Bible Commentary*, vol. 8 (Nashville: Abingdon Press, 1995), 204.

7. For more on this tempter, or "prosecutor," see David Finnegan-Hosey, *Christ on the Psych Ward*, 121–123.

assumed the literal, material meaning of the word "debt," needing an added explanation to emphasize the metaphorical meaning of interpersonal harm and the need for reparation, forgiveness, and reconciliation after said harm.

Debt was an immediate concern for Jesus's listeners. Ivoni Richter Reimer argues that "to speak of debts is to speak of impoverishment, of the lack of conditions for life in abundance." Reimer describes the "principal factors in the growing impoverishment of the population in the time of Jesus" as "debts, taxes, and war," realities of life under Roman occupation for Jesus's first-century Jewish community.[8] In her commentary on the prayer of Jesus in the Gospel of Luke, Sharon Ringe notes that "it is a prayer most appropriate to persons living in a time and place of frequent famines, undependable harvests, and economic exploitation of the poor, such as was the case for Jesus and his followers, and for many in Luke's church as well."[9] Ringe goes on to comment on Luke's use of both the words for "sin" and "debt," relating it to the theme of the Jubilee or "Year of the Lord's Favor" that runs throughout Luke's Gospel. The very first sermon that Jesus preaches in a synagogue in his hometown of Nazareth is based in a passage from Isaiah about the Jubilee, in which good news to the poor involves "'release' or 'forgiveness,' both of monetary debts and of other expressions of captivity or enslavement," of which we are to be both grateful recipients and generous givers.[10] Debt, and the system of power and control which surrounds it, is no "First World Problem," but a first-century problem. In fact, it's older even than that.

Long before Jesus's earthly ministry, his Jewish ancestors were convinced of the divine importance of dealing with injustices surrounding a system of debt and debtors. Walter Brueggemann posits that a commandment about the forgiveness of material debts in Deuteronomy 15 represents the most important command in the Torah:

---

8. Ivoni Richter Reimer, "The Forgiveness of Debts in Matthew and Luke: For an Economy without Exclusion," in *Voices from the Margin: Interpreting the Bible in the Third World*, 3rd ed., ed. R. S. Sugirtharajah (Maryknoll: Orbis, 2006), 145.

9. Sharon H. Ringe, *Luke* (Louisville: Westminster John Knox Press, 1995), 163.

10. Ringe, *Luke*, 164–65.

I'll give you a little Hebrew grammar—I know you've been waiting
for this. Biblical Hebrew has no adverbs. The way it expresses the
intensity of the verb, it repeats the verb. So if it says give and you want
to say "really give" it says "give give" right in the sentence—"give give."
This law about the Year of Release—there are five absolute infin-
itives that you can't spot in English. There are more intense verbs
in this law than anywhere else in the Old Testament. This is Moses
saying, "I mean this."[11]

Brueggemann's claim that the grammatical structure of Hebrew makes
this the *most* important commandment in the Torah is admittedly
hyperbolic, likely designed more as a rhetorical emphasis than a literal
argument. Nevertheless, he makes the point that the Jewish Scriptures,
which would have been the Scriptures of Jesus and his early followers,
are deeply concerned about the potentially damaging effects and economic injustice of crushing debt. And of course, the Jubilee year that
Jesus refers to in his synagogue sermon in Luke's Gospel, and which the
prayer he teaches his disciples makes reference to, is commanded by the
Jewish Torah. Leviticus 25 set up a cycle in which, every fifty years, "the
Jubilee laws required that the land be granted a year of rest (a "fallow"
year, when no crops would be sown); *debts were to be canceled*; and any
Israelite who had become an indentured servant would be set free.[12]

Throughout the Torah, the people of God are instructed to regularly forgive debts, to free each other of financial obligations, bondage,
and servitude. Jesus, deeply rooted in the tradition of his Jewish ancestors and contemporaries, teaches his disciples a prayer for forgiveness
of debts which, by metaphorical extension, is a prayer for release from
other forms of accumulated injustice and harm.

The entirety of this rushing river of ancient tradition flowed
beneath my impromptu conversation with a young adult about

---

11. Walter Brueggemann, Barton Clinton-Gordey Lecture Series at Boston Ave-
nue United Methodist Church, February 2012, as cited by Jeremy Smith, "The Most
Important Command in the Old Testament isn't what you think," *Hacking Christianity* blog, December 6, 2013, available online: *http://hackingchristianity.net/2013/12/
the-most-important-command-in-the-old-testament.html*.

12. Ringe, *Luke*, 68. Emphasis added.

different versions of the Lord's Prayer and brought home for me the relevance of this simple act of worship on the material struggle that was occupying much of my mental and emotional energy. I was reminded that Jesus's prayer is an old, old prayer with surprising relevance for a contemporary issue: an ancient-modern prayer for an ancient-modern problem. From that day on, I began praying the prayer Jesus taught with the words, "Forgive us our debts, as we forgive our debtors." The words had new meaning to me, both in the literal sense and also, because of my visceral connection to the burden of debt, in their metaphorical sense. The palpable reality of actual debt in my life made the individual and interpersonal aspect of forgiveness even more vivid. To this day, when I pray the prayer Jesus taught to the disciples so long ago, I pray for forgiveness from debts.

Debt, Forgiveness, and Salvation

This conversation about debts and forgiveness in Jesus's prayer highlights yet another connection between our God-talk and the language we use to talk about mental healthcare in the United States. For Christians, concepts of forgiveness, grace, and salvation are deeply intertwined. What would it mean to take seriously the forgiveness of debt as one aspect of God's gracious, saving work?

A few years ago, I was singing a congregational hymn in worship that included a line about Jesus paying our debt, a reference to one traditional form of atonement theology in which Jesus's death on the cross is understood as paying our debt of sin.[13] I had a strange experience of contradiction as I sang. On the one hand, I have a theological bone to pick with this style of atonement theology, which often, at least in its modern form, tends to isolate Jesus's death from his life and ministry, glorifies violent sacrifice, and can make salvation into an entirely individualistic spiritualized experience which, as you may have picked up on by now, I would argue is not the healthiest or most holistic understanding of the term.

---

13. For more about atonement theology in relation to mental health struggles, see Finnegan-Hosey, *Christ on the Psych Ward*, 26–27.

At the same time, I thought, "Wow. I just got out of significant, concrete, financial debt because of a strong support system, the generosity of others, and a series of surprising events. It's an incredibly freeing feeling. This thing that has been haunting my thoughts is suddenly gone. I feel free and grateful, and I feel inspired to be more generous and a better steward of my resources. My debt literally got paid."

And I wonder if that feeling, that experience, is meant to be evoked by biblical passages about Jesus's payment of our debts, rather than to be read as an argument about the systematic theology of atonement. For people who have had first-hand experience with the crushing weight of real debt, a debt being paid off by a third party would be good news indeed. And it would certainly seem to point to a community of faith that took the forgiveness of actual debts, the biblical Jubilee, as seriously as it took individual acts of repentance, reparation, and forgiveness. We can argue all day about what it might mean to talk about Jesus paying our debt, but if the body of Christ isn't part of freeing people from debt, right now, then all of the words on all sides of that argument are likely to ring hollow.

The good news is that there are numerous ways communities of faith can be part of freeing people from debt in the here and now. A recent article in *USA Today*, for example, tells the story of a number of congregations that have helped eliminate millions of dollars of medical debt by raising money for the non-profit RIP Medical Debt, an organization that "buys debt portfolios on this secondary market for pennies on the dollar with money from its donors. But instead of collecting the debt, RIP forgives it."[14] Since "hospitals and doctors are eager to get those hard-to-collect debts off their books, they sell them cheap," which means donations from churches and other sources can have an outsized impact in forgiving outstanding medical debts.[15] RIP Medical Debt got its start as an outgrowth of an

---

14. Roxie Hammill, Kaiser Health News, "Millions in crushing medical debt—gone. All thanks to these churches," *USA Today*, May 31, 2019, available online: *https://www.usatoday.com/story/news/2019/05/31/church-pays-medical-bills-debt-rip-medical-debt/1286600001/*.

15. Hammill, "Millions in crushing medical debt—gone," *USA Today*.

Occupy Wall Street–related effort to forgive debts, and while that particular initiative now focuses on student loan forgiveness, RIP Medical Debt continues its original mission.[16] The name of that original initiative? Rolling Jubilee—a direct reference to the biblical Jubilee which Jesus's prayer, with its petition for the forgiveness of debts, points to.[17]

Of course, though such debt relief can offer freedom for individuals, broader structural issues remain. *USA Today* notes several recent efforts to address the larger issue: "The federal Consumer Financial Protection Bureau proposed a rule in May to curb debt collectors' ability to bug those with outstanding bills, and some states have tried various measures, such as limiting the interest rates collectors may charge."[18] A number of presidential candidates have suggested plans to tackle other forms of debt such as student loan forgiveness or predatory loans. The Poor People's Campaign, which organizes in collaboration with many faith communities and faith leaders, includes in its demands related to poverty and inequality "relief from crushing household, student, and consumer debt," and adds, "We declare Jubilee."[19]

Faith communities can join in efforts to alleviate the stress and pain of crushing debts caused by needed healthcare, including mental healthcare. They can understand this work as a key part of their participation in the *missio Dei*, the mission of God in the world. Salvation, in a holistic sense, means healing and wholeness. If forgiveness of debts and forgiveness of sins are intertwined, and if forgiveness, in the Christian understanding, is a key component of salvation, then part of the healing salve of God's grace is the healing of economic wounds. To be saved includes being liberated from debt and economic injustice.

---

16. "What is RIP Medical Debt?," video available online at: *www.ripmedicaldebt.org/*.

17. *https://rollingjubilee.org/*.

18. Hammill, "Millions in crushing medical debt—gone," *USA Today*.

19. Poor People's Campaign, "A Moral Agenda Based on Fundamental Rights," available online: *www.poorpeoplescampaign.org/demands/*.

I still pray the prayer Jesus taught with the words, "Forgive us our debts." Now, when I say these words, I reflect gratefully on the alleviation of my own debt. I also reflect on my own role, and the role of my faith community, in participating in the divine work of forgiving debts and declaring Jubilee. More than that, I think about the powerful structures that hide behind the overt impacts of something like the debt crisis. The prayer that Jesus taught speaks to those powers when it evokes the "reign" or "kingdom of God," and when it petitions for salvation from "the Evil One." All of this vocabulary is New Testament language for what we today might call "systems."

PART

2

Systems

We are saved *by* pre-existing grace,
from unhealthy systems,
for the common good.

If grace is not only for the individual and salvation encompasses healing, wholeness, and liberation, then to speak of grace saving us also means to speak of those forces and realities that seek to impede the work of grace and keep us unhealthy, fragmented, and entrapped. It is imperative to broaden the conversation as we work to break the silence, challenge stigma, and share our own stories of mental illness, mental health, and recovery. To share my own story and to witness to the sufficiency of grace within the pain of that story is also to begin speaking of the systems and barriers that prevent access to care for so many in this country.

Talking about systems does not only mean analyzing concrete examples of injustice or dissecting policy. Systems are also spiritual. Theologian Walter Wink began studying the New Testament language of power in the 1980s while witnessing the response of the Latin American church to human rights violations and dictatorial abuses. He argues that the "principalities and powers" that concerned the New Testament writers were "the inner and outer aspects of any given manifestations of power," not only the "tangible manifestations which power takes" but also "the spirituality of institutions, the 'within' of corporate structures and systems, the inner essence of outer organizations of power."[1] As an example of the operation of this New

---

1. Walter Wink, *The Powers,* vol. 1: *Naming the Powers: The Language of Power in the New Testament* (Philadelphia: Fortress Press, 1984), 5.

Testament language of power, Wink points to the language in the first
and second chapter of Ephesians that sets the stage for the epistle writer's theology of grace.[2]

The author of Ephesians explicitly places the gospel of grace in
the context of Jesus's triumph over the powers of the world, with
"by grace you have been saved" immediately preceding the statement that God has "raised us up with Christ and seated us with
God in the heavenly places in Christ Jesus" (Ephesians 2:5–6). This
is a direct reference to a prior verse about God raising Jesus, not
only from the dead, but above earthly powers: "God put this power
to work in Christ when God raised him from the dead and seated
him at his right hand in the heavenly places, far above all rule and
authority and power and dominion, and above every name that is
named, not only in this age but also in the age to come" (Ephesians
1:20–21). Biblical scholar E. Elizabeth Johnson notes that while
the author of Ephesians "is careful to locate believers' resurrection
with Christ in the eschatological future," the letter "says that Christians have already been raised with Christ and therefore currently
share his heavenly home." This makes the "Pauline slogan in 2:5,8
('by grace you have been saved') . . . a development beyond Paul,
for whom salvation is always a future reality" rather than the heavenly
present reality of Ephesians.[3]

Raised with Christ above the powers. This language is how biblical writers grapple with broken systems and with the way that God's
grace made manifest in Jesus Christ challenges, upends, and ultimately
heals them. Delving into the language of power in Ephesians 1:20–23,
in which the risen Christ sits at God's right hand above the powers
and principalities, Wink writes that the Ephesian church "could see
that they had been living in the shackles of inauthentic behavior not
even entirely of their own choosing. . . . They had, in short, been
captives, and now were to an astonishing measure free. . . . The

---

2. Ibid., 60–64, 82–84.

3. E. Elizabeth Johnson, "Ephesians," in *Women's Bible Commentary: Revised and
Updated,* 3rd edition, ed. Carol A. Newsom, Sharon H. Ringe, and Jacqueline E. Lapsley (Louisville: Westminster John Knox, 2012), 577.

"new creation" is already in process of being established."[4] Christ, who according to Ephesians has in some mysterious sense already transformed the harmful systems of this world, communicates grace to a world in need of it. To speak of grace is also to witness to these systems with the faith that they are already subject to transformation.

---

4. Wink, *Naming the Powers*, 63.

4

Mental Illness Isn't Violence (But Our Systems Sure Are Sick)

I wish I didn't have to talk about violence in a book about mental illness. I wish I didn't have to run the risk, even inadvertently, of reinforcing the stereotype that connects mental illness with violence, particularly with mass shootings in the United States. But if I don't talk about it, the vacuum left by silence gets filled with a cacophony of misdirection. So I have to talk about it, even though I don't want to, even though I worry that even raising the subject reinforces exactly the association that I want to challenge and critique.

Let me tell you how this goes for me. I hear the news or see it in that early morning social media check that I keep telling myself I should stop doing. "Oh, no," I say, softly, to myself. I try to stop for a second, before I react, before I think. It rarely works, but I try. I try to just shut up for a second. To extend empathy and compassion out into the universe. I try to imagine the unimaginable. I try to feel, at least for a moment, some of the terror that the people on the scene must have felt. It is a vain attempt, of course. I try, and I fail.

Sometimes, I cry. Other times, I'm simply numb. And sometimes the news of yet another mass shooting just fades into the background noise, normalized in the most terrifying of ways by the endless cycle of trauma and crisis marching down through our collective news feed.

"There's been another one."

How terrible to be able to say, "Another one." Another name, another place, in the litany of mass shootings in this country. "Another one." How blasphemous that we keep saying that. How horrific.

"The deadliest." We say that again, too. Of course, it's only true if we ignore other horrors, other massacres whose blood is still dried on our hands. But even if we add some qualifiers, I wish we'd stop saying "the deadliest." Every bullet that invades a body, that kicks down the doors of skin to stop a heart, breaks countless more. Every sacrifice to this false God is the deadliest for someone, some family, some child, some friend.

The deadliest, the deadliest. Who cares about the number when the blood is still drying on the pavement? That day—whatever day it was, whether children, or Bible-studying elders, or concertgoers—that day the clocks stopped for someone for whom that day will always be the deadliest.

"The deadliest," the reporters say. I react. Then I wait. I don't usually have to wait long to be informed that

> Since this killer was white
> And a male
> And we can find no way to blame his violence on people we are killing in even larger numbers than this latest massacre—
> then
> surely
> he must be insane.

"Mentally ill," they say, as if using medical language makes the insinuation feel less like a knife in my already twisted gut.

I breathe in sharply. The tension rises in my chest. I let myself feel the hurt in my body. In my bones where, I imagine, I can still feel my sickness, even though it hurts me less right now, scares me less. Just for a moment. Just for a moment. I hold the silence, just for a little while. I breathe in. I breathe out. I breathe in. I remember what words will fill that silence if I don't speak up. And so I do.

Being Honest about Illness and Violence

I have a mental illness. That's something you know, since you've read this far. I have bipolar disorder. Type II, if you're into those kinds of details. That does not make me statistically more likely to commit a violent act than anyone else (and not just because I'm an aspiring pacifist). According to the U.S. Department of Health and Human Services, only 3–5 percent of violent acts can be attributed to people with serious mental illnesses. The same source reports that people with severe mental illness are more than ten times more likely to be victims of violent crime than other people.[1] And yet, according to researchers from Johns Hopkins, more than one out of two articles on popular news sites that mention mental illness also mention violence, fueling (and being fueled by) a public perception that mental illness correlates with violence.[2] I worry that this very chapter contributes to that same phenomenon. And I've seen this correlation play out personally. At my seminary, after students pushed the administration to provide more resources related to mental health and mental illness, one of the first responses of the administration was to provide training for RAs on dealing with someone with a mental illness who was acting violently. It was seen as the most important first step, preceding the provision of support or resources for students struggling with mental health challenges, many of whom were suffering in silence. Despite the inaccuracy of the perceived link between violence and mental health struggles, and its stigmatizing nature, it has proven to have a lot of staying power.

There are a few important clarifications to make about this general information. One is that "mental illness" is not one thing. The term is used for a bunch of different diagnoses, which in turn are based on a bunch of different presenting symptoms. I've written before about diagnoses as stories we tell to make sense of human experiences, an idea some people might be surprised to learn I got from one of my psychiatrists.[3] Some of these particular diagnoses include as particular symptoms

---

1. "Mental Health Myths and Facts," *MentalHealth.gov,* August 29, 2017, available online: *https://www.mentalhealth.gov/basics/mental-health-myths-facts.*

2. Alexandra Sifferlin, "Most Violent Crimes Are Wrongly Linked to Mental Illness," *Time,* June 6, 2016, available online: *https://time.com/4358295/violent-crimes-mental-illness/.*

3. See David Finnegan-Hosey, *Christ on the Psych Ward* (New York: Church Publishing, 2018), 107–25.

feelings or urges or compulsions toward violence, which is important to acknowledge because these types of feelings can be incredibly scary, and the silence and stigma around them can keep people from seeking help.

When I admitted myself into the hospital in 2011, I was asked several times during the admissions process if I felt like I wanted to hurt myself (I most certainly did; that's why I was there) and if I wanted to hurt anyone else (I did not, though I made a snarky remark about my internet service provider). Those questions are standard because mental health struggles can include these kinds of thoughts. In my case, these compulsions were directed toward myself. That's not the case for everyone. These kinds of urges and compulsions are very scary for people. They're called "intrusive thoughts" because that's just what they do: intrude, even invade, a mind that does not want them there.

But having intrusive thoughts is not the same thing as going out and buying dozens of firearms and then meticulously planning a mass shooting. While some mass shootings have been carried out by people with mental illnesses, because mental illness is actually relatively common in the general population, the number isn't statistically significant. About one in five people have some form of diagnosable mental illness at some point in their lifetime. Much more significant as a common denominator across most mass shootings is white men with guns.

Another important clarification involves a sort of instinct or gut feeling that people have when such a shooting occurs, that is articulated like this: "Whether or not this person had some sort of diagnosis, surely a mentally healthy person would not do something like this?" That has a certain logic. Shouldn't being willing to shoot hundreds of people in and of itself constitute some sort of unhealthy mindset? But there are problems with this reasoning. For one thing, it's a circular argument. If you define "willing to commit violence" as a mental health problem, then—ta-da—every act of violence is committed by someone with a mental health problem. The premise proves itself.

More importantly, however, the actual effect of such reasoning is, first, to continue the stigmatizing of those with mental illness; second, to give us an easy out from having difficult conversations about guns; third, to dodge all the other issues involved such as toxic masculinity and white supremacy; all while, fourth, to not actually help people with mental health issues, because—and this is important—if we only bring up the brokenness of this country's mental healthcare system after a shooting, we make zero progress, and we reinforce the stigma that prevents us from making progress in the first place.

But—and here's the clarification, which gets us, I think, closer to the crux of the matter—there's some wisdom in wanting to name mass violence as a mentally unhealthy thing (as well as emotionally and spiritually, not to mention physically). If we want to talk about violence as a form of illness, a form of dis-ease, that's fine. Let's talk about it. It's just that mental illness, which deals with an individual's struggle with experiences that prevent them from functioning the way they want to function, is the wrong category for such a naming. Violence represents a systemic un-health, an interaction between an individual and larger forces that are harmful, that are in and of themselves violent. Such unhealthy systems impact our health—mental, physical, emotional, and spiritual—but that doesn't mean they can be diagnosed by pathologizing an individual.

Mental illness isn't violence, but violence might well be an illness, and a systemic one at that. We've got some very sick systems that are indeed in need of diagnoses.

Systems and the Powers That Be

Diagnosing systems means reckoning with the ways in which unhealthy structures and forms of power impact the health and functioning of individuals within a system or society. Many practitioners of pastoral care recognize the impact of systems on the individuals they care for, which in turn leads to an assessment of these systems and a less individualist, more communal understanding of both pathology and care. Cedric C. Johnson in *Race, Religion, and Resilience in the Neoliberal Age* writes of the need for a diagnostic approach which takes into account material systems and the impact they have on the souls of those caught in them. The plan for care which emerges from this approach, "prophetic soul care," challenges the material systems of injustice and simultaneously seeks the soul-level healing of the person through the "restoration of the *imago dei* . . . the restoration of self-hood, recovery of culture, and resistance against forces that would attempt to deny a people's sense of self and self-determination."[4] This form of healing calls for an "integrative approach" to care within systems, which "entails assessing interpersonal dynamics, family systems, sociocultural systems outside the family, economic and political systems, as well as religious, spiritual, or other meaning-making systems . . . [and] thus requires one to "think systems" at all times, even if the practitioner of care is seeing only one member of a family.[5]

Johnson pictures these various systems as a series of concentric circles, with interpersonal dynamics at the center, surrounded in expanding spheres by family systems, sociocultural systems, political and economic systems, and religious, spiritual, and meaning-making systems, creating a "multi-systems framework for an integrative approach" to care that all interact with and impact each other.[6] The behaviors, strengths, and pathologies of an individual are affected by the multiple systems they operate in, and vice versa. To speak only of an individual pathology or disorder, then, is to miss out on the larger context of the person and the various systems by which they are impacted and which they, in turn, impact.

The reality of multiple interacting systems remains true even for people, such as myself, who really do have a diagnosed mental illness or mood disorder. In *Resurrecting the Person: Friendship and the Care of People with Mental Health Problems,* John Swinton writes of mental illnesses as experiences of complex individuals within complex communities, which "rather than being definable in terms of biology or diagnosis, are an ultimately indefinable combination of pathology, personhood, and community. . . . If we omit one from our caring equation, we risk misunderstanding the others."[7] A diagnosis is only one aspect of a complex human, in community, impacted by systems.

---

4. Cedric C. Johnson, *Race, Religion, and Resilience in the Neoliberal Age* (New York: Palgrave Macmillan, 2016), 7.

5. Ibid., 6.

6. Ibid., 7.

7. John Swinton, *Resurrecting the Person: Friendship and the Care of People with Mental Health Problems* (Nashville: Abingdon, 2000), 27.

We can't just say, "X person had a mental illness" as if that explains their behavior or their personhood. It's an oversimplification and an ineffective and stigmatizing one at that. When we're talking about systems, we're talking about the relationships, communities, and broader forces that impact, and are impacted by, the actions of individuals.

The Bible describes these interacting forces, although its language has been obscured in translation over the time and distance between us and the ancient texts. Let's circle back to Walter Wink's understanding of "spiritual powers," which are not "separate heavenly or ethereal entities" as much as "the inner aspect of material or tangible manifestations of power."[8] Though the biblical language is far from systematic and is often hard to understand, we can recognize patterns, "terms that cluster and swarm around the reality they describe, as if by heaping up synonymous phrases and parallel constructions an intuitive sense of the reality described might emerge."[9]

The letter to the Ephesians includes several examples of this swarming language of power, and indeed such clusters of language in the letter lead precisely to the famous summary of the gospel of grace: "by grace you have been saved." Wink translates the beginning of the second chapter of Ephesians in such a way as to make the language of power more evident, highlighting words whose common translations obscure their connection to the wider vocabulary of power. The opening lines which frame the epistle writer's discussion of grace, according to Wink, are a description of an entire "world system" which, though unseen, surrounds and influences the audience of the letter in the same way the air we breathe surrounds and fills us even though it remains invisible to us. We breathe the toxic air of the powers—"the ruler of the power of the air," as Ephesians names it—and, "having taken in its deadly vapors, we breathe them out on others; we become its carriers, passing it into our institutions, structures, and systems even as these have reciprocally passed on the same deadly fumes to us."[10]

---

8. Walter Wink, *The Powers*, vol. 1: *Naming the Powers: The Language of Power in the New Testament* (Philadelphia: Fortress Press, 1984), 104.

9. Ibid., 99–100.

10. Ibid., 83–84.

The powers cannot simply be reduced to "nothing but" materiality; they have an inward, spiritual component. It is not just that systems don't work, or are designed to cause harm, or fail to function for the good of all. It is that they are alienated or, we might say, spiritually sick. These powers and systems have the sickness of violence that needs to be diagnosed. This diagnosis must take into account broader societal systems and structures in order for a truly healing approach to be possible. Responses to violence which seek to blame individual pathology miss this crucial point and, as a result, leave us captive to the very violence of the systems which entrap us.

Sick Systems, Not a Sick Person

Many sick systems need to be diagnosed in order to prevent horrific acts of mass violence in this country. We must begin the painful process of naming these systems, however incomplete or inadequate our naming might be.[11]

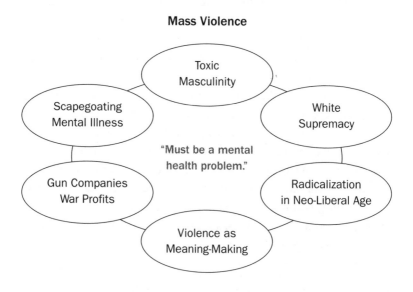

Mass Violence

---

11. "Mass Violence," chart created by Peter Jarrett-Schell. Used by permission.

Toxic Masculinity

The vast majority of acts of mass violence are committed by men. White men commit the majority of mass shootings in the United States.[12] There's a strong correlation between men who commit acts of mass violence and those who have a previous history of domestic violence or abuse against women.[13] Why? Jay Yoder, a community organizer and advocate against sexual violence, writes:

> Masculinity is all the ideas about what being a man means that we've decided as a culture are true and important and necessary. So: being a man means being strong, violent, aggressive. Being a man means being in charge. Etc. etc. etc. . . . [But it] isn't essential for men to be any of these specific things in order to be "worthy" men. When we demand certain things of someone because of what gender we need them to be, and in the case of manhood, when we punish it with ridicule, shame, violence, degradation, humiliation (see frat rituals, team rituals, etc.), it creates a toxic masculinity that is bound up in and enforced by violence.[14]

When we teach men, and, before that, when we teach young boys, that being a man means being dominant, aggressive, and in control, it has consequences. When those young boys grow into men and find out that they can't, in fact, always be strong, always be in control, always win, it has consequences. Violent consequences.

White Supremacy, Race, and Racism

As already noted, mass shootings in the United States correlate not just with masculinity but, more often than not, with white masculinity. On

---

12. John Haltiwanger, "White Men Have Committed More Mass Shootings Than Any Other Group," *Newsweek*, October 2, 2017, available online: *https://www.newsweek.com/white-men-have-committed-more-mass-shootings-any-other-group-675602*.

13. Mark Berman, "The persistent crime that connects mass shooters and terror suspects: Domestic violence," *Post Nation*, August 15, 2017, available online: *https://www.washingtonpost.com/news/post-nation/wp/2017/08/15/the-persistent-crime-that-connects-mass-shooters-and-terror-suspects-domestic-violence/*.

14. Jay Yoder, "Say it with me: Toxic. White. Masculinity.," *QueerPGH*, October 9, 2017, available online: *http://www.queerpgh.com/say-toxic-white-masculinity/*.

August 12, 2012, my wife Leigh and I went to Charlottesville, answering a call from a group of faith leaders called Congregate Charlottesville in response to a major white nationalist rally being organized in the city. We saw the ideology of white supremacy in its blatant, unmasked form, overt violence that resulted in the death of activist Heather Heyers and the injury of many others. At one point, Leigh and I were helping to drive a chaplain to the UVA Hospital to provide care for people being brought in with physical injuries and psychic trauma. On one corner, a group of white nationalist protestors had gathered, armed with guns and clubs. Many had their shirts off, revealing swastika tattoos. They chanted: "White Power! White Power! White Power!"

This open display of white nationalism was an overt manifestation of the more subtle and systemic existence of white supremacy. Rev. William Barber of the Poor People's Campaign points to the difference between "cultural racism," those overt words and symbols which we most often associate with racism, and "systemic [and] policy racism like voter suppression, mass incarceration, resegregation of high poverty schools, attacks on immigrants, attacks on native people," which inscribe racism within the structures and systems of power.[15] Justice educator Alicia Crosby offers this broader definition of white supremacy, which stretches beyond the overt white nationalism of neo-Nazis and KKK members:

> White supremacy establishes whiteness as superior to other racial identities through the elevation of the needs, wants, concerns, perspectives, feelings, and desires of white people over that of people of color. This includes the centering of the theological, rhetorical, aesthetic, and economic priorities and preferences rooted in whiteness as well as the appropriation and rebranding of cultural expressions sourced from people of color.[16]

---

15. William Barber, Clip of "Poor People's Campaign Presidential Forum," 34:00, *C-SPAN,* June 17, 2019, available online: *https://www.c-span.org/video/?c4804117/clip&start=2032.*

16. Alicia T. Crosby, "Recapping Whitewashed Conference Culture: My Reflection on Dialogue About Race in Progressive Christian Spaces," *Patheos.com,* October 9, 2016, *https://www.patheos.com/blogs/aliciacrosby/2016/10/whitewashed-christian-space/.*

White supremacy is a double-edged sword. It teaches white people that we deserve to succeed, that we deserve to be in charge, that we are supposed to be the most successful and most important and the peak of civilization. And when we aren't—when we fail at things, and we lose jobs, and we mess things up, and we're sort of mediocre most of the time just like most other people are, and because we've been taught (often subconsciously, sometimes overtly) that by virtue of the color of our skins we are supposed to be superior, and we don't feel very superior at all, we experience this unnamed type of shame. Stir that in with toxic masculinity and violence very quickly becomes a way to reassert this felt need for control, for success, for extraordinaryness, that is falsely promised to us by white supremacy. Which makes young white men susceptible not only to individual acts of violence, but to intentional radicalization and recruitment.

Radicalization and Recruitment in the Neoliberal Age

The terms radicalization and recruitment are "othered" words in the United States, words we associate with distant countries or "foreign" cultures. But Charlottesville revealed the reality of the radicalization of young, white Americans, many of whom are perceived as, and experience themselves as, "losers" and how certain extremist groups take advantage of that perceived experience.[17] Julie Norman and Drew Mikhael draw connections between their research on youth radicalization in the Middle East and North Africa and the Charlottesville attack:

> From our focus groups, youths who were the most susceptible to radical messaging were those who perceived themselves to be politically and/or economically marginalized, resulting in a pervasive sense of purposelessness and lack of hope for the future. However, it was not poor socio-economic status itself that pointed toward

---

17. German Lopez, "The radicalization of white Americans," August 18, 2017, *Vox*, available online: *https://www.vox.com/identities/2017/8/18/16151924/radicalization-white-supremacists-nazis.*

susceptibility, but rather a sense of relative deprivation, coupled with feelings of political and/or social exclusion.[18]

If you've been told that you're supposed to be in control, and successful, and in charge, but instead you feel excluded, or like a failure, or like a loser . . . well, it's that much easier for you to radicalize yourself on the internet, or to be intentionally radicalized by a particular organization.

The folks who are most susceptible to this are the cast-offs of what Johnson calls the neoliberal age,[19] the ones who have been promised much but offered little. And so they go looking for something that can provide them meaning, purpose, a sense of superiority or at least of value. Norman and Mikhael again:

> Ideology matters, but not necessarily its core messaging, be it Islamic fundamentalism or white supremacy. Rather, radical groups use religion and ideologies to legitimize grievances, placing themselves as agents of change and promising empowerment and a sense of purpose.[20]

And if you're looking for meaning and purpose and power in this culture, there's no promise more alluring than the meaning-making power of violence.

A Culture of Violence, or, Violence as Meaning-Making System

The outermost of Cedric Johnson's concentric circles of interacting systems is "Religious, Spiritual, and Meaning-Making Systems."

---

18. Julie M. Norman and Drew Mikhael, "Youth radicalization is on the rise. Here's what we know about why," *The Washington Post*, August 28, 2017, *https:// www.washingtonpost.com/news/monkey-cage/wp/2017/08/25/youth-radicalization-is-on-the-rise-heres-what-we-know-about-why/?utm_term=.ce25e5418715*.

19. Johnson defines the neoliberal age as "the emergence of a hegemonic configuration driven by neoliberal ideas, but permeated by a myriad of other forces . . . [which] involves a matrix of systems that function to: (1) *maintain* the full reign of the 'free' market, (2) *contain* left behind sectors of the population whose presence discloses the systems' inequities, (3) *control* those populations who pose a threat to the systems' stability, and (4) secure the continued *contributions* of those who are indeed indispensable to the system's operations." Johnson, *Race, Religion, and Resilience*, 48.

20. Norman and Mikhael, "Youth radicalization," *The Washington Post*.

Ideologies like white supremacy can fill this role, but I would argue that in our country, violence itself functions as a meaning-making system. Wink refers to the "Myth of Redemptive Violence," which "enshrines the belief that violence saves, that war brings peace, that might makes right;"[21] while former war correspondent Chris Hedges analyzes the ways in which war functions as "a force that gives us meaning."[22] In a culture of violence, enactments of violence promise meaning, purpose, and power, obscuring the fact that violence gives none of those things. It just gives injury and death.

Gun Companies and War Profiteering

Of course, all of these factors are exacerbated and made more deadly by the ready availability of guns. Groups like Moms Demand Action and Everytown for Gun Safety[23] lobby for legislative changes, which is important; but of course, the biggest obstacle they face is the big money available from the gun lobby and, behind that, from gun companies. The biggest guns in the room, literally and figuratively, are corporations that make billions off of selling weapons. And the U.S. government itself is the biggest buyer of weapons from private companies. We've normalized war profiteering in this country. How are gun companies that sell personal firearms doing anything different from what the military industrial complex has been promoting on a massive, hundreds-of-billions-of-dollars scale? These are big, big, money-making industries that make donations to political campaigns and lobby members of Congress. What's a few dozen dead church members or concertgoers measured against trillions of dollars?

The Stigmatizing and Scapegoating of Mental Illness

The stigmatizing and scapegoating of people with mental illnesses is itself an aspect of the violent systems at play in mass shootings. For

---

21. Walter Wink, *The Powers That Be: Theology for a New Millennium* (New York: Galilee Doubleday, 1998), 42.

22. Chris Hedges, *War is a Force That Gives Us Meaning* (Anchor, 2003).

23. See *https://momsdemandaction.org/* and *https://everytown.org/*.

one thing, people who genuinely do have a mental illness are discouraged from seeking help and sharing their pain because of the stigma. For another, mental illness provides an easy scapegoat and a "pretend" response to violence: we can easily talk about the invisible thing that is mental health, not do anything about it, and allow the violence to continue while patting ourselves on the back about our statements. How many people who talked about mental health after any of our country's mass shootings have genuinely rolled up their sleeves and gotten to work to fix the mental healthcare system? Very few, I suspect. And of course, there is an entire collection of other overlapping systems that directly impact mental healthcare: insurance companies, pharmaceutical companies, national legislation, lack of mental health parity, and more.

All of these forces conspire to cause a widespread level of trauma, a conglomeration of systems that Johnson refers to as a "traumatogenic environment."[24] While not itself a system per se, the collective trauma that results from this alignment of oppressive and violent systems impacts the mental health and well-being of millions of people. This impact is put on gruesome display in the rhetoric that follows in the wake of mass shootings. An event which causes massive trauma is blamed on the mental health of the perpetrator when, ironically, it is the victims of such an incident whose mental health is most compromised. A framework of care, rather than of blame, is called for—and one in which care is framed in terms of systems rather than solely in terms of individuals.

Multiple Systems Are Always at Play . . . So What Do We Do?

I can't hope to provide a complete list of the systems at play, nor an exhaustive diagnosis of each of them. Multiple systems, multiple powers, visible and invisible, are always at play, impacting and being impacted by the actions of individuals, which feels overwhelming. So, what do we do?

---

24. Johnson, *Race, Religion, and Resilience*, 78.

By naming these systems, we begin the process of diagnosing them, treating them, and caring for the people impacted by them. And if it is true, as a psychiatrist once said to me, that diagnoses are stories we tell about a complex web of symptoms and experiences and treatments, then diagnosis and care involves telling a story that leads us toward wholeness and healing.

"Strategies for care," in the words of Cedric Johnson, "are derived from an ongoing assessment of where and how to intervene, whether the practitioner is addressing interpersonal dynamics, family dynamics, or the larger systems within which the person or group exists."[25] John Swinton frames this idea specifically in terms of mental health struggles:

> Mental health problems, rather than being definable in terms of biology or diagnosis, are an ultimately indefinable combination of pathology, personhood, and community; the aspects are inextricably interlinked. If we omit one from our caring equation, we risk misunderstanding the others.[26]

We have to "think systems," to use Johnson's phrase, in order to diagnose systemic pathologies, and violence is one of those systemic pathologies. We have to look at the many different systems impacting a particular person or situation, knowing that we might miss things, that we probably can't understand the whole picture with 100 percent accuracy. And then we choose where to intervene, where to put energy, where to try to affect the system, while being mindful of the intersections and interactions between our interventions and other parts of the system.

We certainly need to be advocating for better mental healthcare. It's a big part of my own calling and a big part of the reason I am writing this book. But we also need to keep in mind the broader contexts. We need to look at how race and gender, how racism and sexism, all impact mental health, and to understand how associating mental illness with violence reinscribes stigma. We think systems, we choose

---

25. Ibid., 6–7.

26. Swinton, *Resurrecting the Person,* 27.

an intervention, we act, and we assess the system again. Mental illness isn't violence, but our systems do create a lot of violence, and our conversation about mental health and mental healthcare in this country ought to include an analysis of the many systems that impact an individual who is struggling with mental health.

On "Thoughts and Prayers"

Recently, after acts of mass violence in this country, a weird online debate swirled around the appropriateness (or lack thereof) of offering "thoughts and prayers." A big part of it is a reaction to the hypocrisy of "leaders" who take money from gun lobbyists and refuse to take any real action against gun violence. From these leaders, "thoughts and prayers" does indeed sound like an empty phrase, the useless clanging of a gong. This debate has been even more pronounced when shootings happen in churches while people are praying and worshiping.

It's difficult for me to enter into this conversation. My heart feels too heavy after news of mass violence, too heavy to engage in the back and forth of hot-takes, think pieces, and social media battles. News of tragedy can feel paralyzing. What do we do in the face of such violence? What could possibly be an appropriate response? And will my hurting, heartfelt response in turn become a site of internet debate and controversy when I am feeling particularly emotionally raw and unequipped to engage in such things?

As a person of faith, I believe prayer is an appropriate response to tragedy. We join together in prayer for all victims of violence and for all those mourning the dead. We pray for peace and for justice. We pray that God will stir up in us a concern for our common humanity and a love for neighbor, even a love for those who would declare themselves our enemies. We take a moment to intentionally extend our compassion to those in pain, even and especially because many of them are strangers to us. But is prayer enough?

In one obvious sense, no. Prayer is not enough. Action is needed. But in another sense, prayer, rightly understood, is enough. For Christians, the spirituality we express in prayer is an orientation toward and a communion with Jesus Christ. This Jesus to whom we pray is called Emmanuel, "God with us." This Jesus stands in solidarity with all those who are victimized and oppressed, all those who are hurting and mourning, all those who are afflicted and sorely pressed. When we read the story of the Crucifixion, we are reminded that in Christ God stands in solidarity even with those who feel forsaken or abandoned by God. When we pray, we open ourselves up to the movement of the Spirit of Christ, which is always the Spirit of solidarity, of reconciliation, and of love in action. Prayer is an expression of solidarity that leads us into further action; and, conversely, our actions of solidarity and advocacy are expressions of prayer.

When I pray aloud, something I am often called upon to do in my role as a college chaplain, I often conclude by saying, "When we don't know how to pray, God's Spirit cries out within us in sighs too deep for words." I didn't invent this phrase. It is an adaptation of the words of the Apostle Paul, from his letter to the church in Rome: "Likewise, the Spirit helps us in our weakness; for we do not know how to pray as we ought, but that very Spirit intercedes with sighs too deep for words. And God, who searches the heart, knows what is the mind of the Spirit, because the Spirit intercedes for the saints according to the will of God" (Romans 8:26–27).

Just before those lines, Paul writes of hope in the midst of the suffering of creation: "We know that the whole creation has been groaning in labor pains until now; and not only the creation, but we ourselves, who have the first fruits of the Spirit, groan inwardly while we wait for adoption, the redemption of our bodies. For in hope we were saved. Now hope that is seen is not hope. For who hopes for what is seen? But if we hope for what we do not see, we wait for it with patience" (Romans 8:22–25).

All creation is groaning with strife. After a mass shooting or act of violence, we hear those groans in a profound and painful way. In the face of such division and tragedy, it is often difficult to know how to pray, much less what to do. Yet Paul links the groaning of creation in the midst of suffering with the groaning of our own hearts in prayer. When we join together in prayer for those who are hurting, we link ourselves to the cries of creation and find ourselves in the heart of God.[27] Prayer links us to Christ in solidarity with the groaning of creation. Prayer is solidarity. And solidarity is prayer.

One of the central tasks of the Christian community is to proclaim good news—and it is difficult, sometimes seemingly impossible, to do so when faced with such a proliferation of tragic news. Yet, in the midst of the suffering of creation, there is something being born, something being brought to life: the hoped-for redemption, not only of humanity, but of the cosmos. And so we pray, and we act. In the words of hymn writer Fred Kaan: "For the healing of the nations, Lord, we pray with one accord; for a just and equal sharing of the things that earth affords; to a life of love in action help us rise and pledge our word."[28] Our prayers join together with the prayers of the world, with the groaning of creation, and lead us out into the world as a sign of solidarity and love in action. And as we go into the world, to love and to work, we are reminded of Jesus's promise: "And remember, I am with you always, to the end of the age" (Matthew 28:20).

By all means, send thoughts and send prayers. Send prayers by extending real compassion to the people who have been hurt and killed. Pray for the wisdom and the insight to know how to respond responsibly. And put your thoughts to work. Put your mind to work. Think about systems. Think about the multiple factors that impact a person to lead them to violence. And think carefully and prayerfully—what the Christian tradition has referred to as "discernment"—about how you, too, and the communities you inhabit, are impacted by and in turn can impact those systems.

Thoughts and prayers? Yes, by all means. Actions? Yes, those too. Putting them all together? That's thinking systems. That's the kind of thing that might just lead us to properly diagnose this problem. And maybe, just maybe, to find a cure.

---

27. Trevor Hudson with Stephen Bryant, *Listening to the Groans: A Spirituality for Ministry and Mission* (Nashville: Upper Room Books, 2007).

28. Fred Kaan, "For the Healing of the Nations" (Hope Publishing, 1968).

5

There (But) for the Grace
of God

It was late winter, one of the coldest nights of the year in Washington, D.C. I was wrapping a scarf around my face as I prepared to lead a group of college students, members of Georgetown University's Hypothermia Outreach Team (HOT), out into that frigid night.[1] As we prepared ourselves for the cold, I gave the final piece of guidance I always offered before we headed out into the night, a line that was starting to feel a bit rehearsed: "We're going to check in with each other throughout the night. If you're feeling cold, or tired, you let the rest of us know, ok? Our goal is to decrease the overall hypothermia rate tonight, not add to it." As usual, I got a few laughs.

On nights when D.C. activated its hypothermia alert, we walked a route around the neighborhood, talking to folks experiencing homelessness. Participating in this effort was not a natural choice for me. I hate being cold, hence all the layers. We checked in on people, encouraging them to seek shelter and connecting them with transportation if they were interested; we would have some snacks and water, some socks and hats, some hand-warmers to give out. If they hadn't heard of our community partner, the Georgetown Ministry Center (GMC), we would give them information about the services offered there. At least once or twice every winter, we called an ambulance for someone

---

1. For more information about Hypothermia Outreach Teams, a collaboration between Georgetown University's Center for Social Justice and the Georgetown Ministry Center, see *https://csj.georgetown.edu/HOMEprogram*; and David Finnegan-Hosey, "On the Coldest Nights," *Georgetown Ministry Center Newsletter,* February 21, 2017, available online: *https://georgetownministrycenter.org/2017/02/21/on-the-coldest-nights/*.

suffering from the first stages of hypothermia. In so many ways, it wasn't much—preventing hypothermia deaths is hardly a long-term solution to homelessness. The hope was always that the consistent outreach provided by GMC and HOT would connect people who otherwise exist largely outside of the city's network of services to housing and longer-term solutions. On many nights, that didn't happen. But we kept going out because on some nights, it did.

As we headed down the hill, students asked me questions. How long have I been doing this? (It was only my second year—I'd been out maybe half a dozen times before.) How likely was it that the people we would be talking to would take our offer of a free ride to a shelter? (Honestly, not likely most nights; folks have stayed out on colder and wetter nights, but it was good to ask just in case, and to keep them connected to their available resources.) And, of course, the question always came up, as well it should: why do people go homeless in Georgetown, one of D.C.'s most affluent neighborhoods?

The answers are complex. There's a lack of affordable and available housing in D.C. People gravitate to Georgetown because, just like the people who live in the beautiful houses lining the old brick sidewalks, they perceive it as safe and quiet. And most of the folks we would be talking to on that night were people who experience chronic homelessness and who usually suffer from either a severe mental illness or chronic addiction issues or both. These weren't folks who had simply lost jobs or been priced out of affordable housing. These were people with multiple challenges. Though, as I always pointed out, there was a chicken-and-egg question: did homelessness cause illness, or illness cause homelessness? Both were true, I suspected, in various degrees and with various people. Individual pathology and systemic brokenness are not easily separated. Lack of available housing and community mental healthcare might worsen the struggle for some people, cause it for others.

Often, the first person we saw was someone whose name I knew. He had never taken the offer of shelter, but was always friendly and thanked us for checking. Students participating for their first time always remarked on how kind and polite he was. More polite, more kind, than a world in which people sleep under bridges in a wealthy neighborhood in a wealthy city in a wealthy country on a night were temperatures dipped below freezing, I always thought. Of course, not everyone we spoke to that night was polite. I didn't blame them. I doubted I would be.

Most of the students on the team didn't know that I struggled with a mental illness. Most of them didn't know that I had as much in common with the man hidden in the alcove who politely declined our offer of shelter, or with the man who told us that the best thing we can do for him was to "just f—k off," or with any of the other folks we spoke to, as I did with them. Just a few (un)lucky ticks on my genetic code, a bit of family support here or an economic buffer there, was all that separated us, though the chasm between us seemed, at times, unfathomably deep.

As we talked to people under bridges, huddled in sleeping bags in storefronts and alcoves, even tent-camping in Washington Circle, I was constantly aware of my own mental illness. Our experiences were different in so many ways, and yet on paper, I shared a diagnosis, a disorder, with many of them. I was much more like the homeless "them" than most of the outreach team "us" realized. These folks were, in some sense, "my people." The fact that I was "doing outreach" while they were the ones "being outreached to" was pure accident. There was a thin line between us, a massive gap of privilege and circumstance. Though we lived in the same neighborhood, we lived in entirely different worlds.

You may have heard the phrase, attributed to the English Reformer John Bradford, who muttered to himself while witnessing the execution of a group of prisoners, "There but for the grace of God go I." The expression is supposed to communicate that our fortune comes by no merit of our own; we have not earned our life. It has been given to us as a gift.

But there is something wrong with that expression, at least in this instance. It is not grace that separates my life from the kind gentleman sleeping under the bridge, who always thanked us for the visit but declined our offer of shelter. It is not grace that separates me from the couple who slept in the tent near the hospital and said they came to

D.C. from Houston after the floods. It is not grace that separates me from the angry man who told us, in no uncertain terms, to leave him the hell alone. If I believe anything, I believe all of these people are as much recipients of God's grace as I am. Look to luck, to privilege, to systemic injustice, or to the contingencies of life on this "not yet" side of heaven's reign if you want an explanation for our circumstances, but do not blame grace.

As I walked around Georgetown in the freezing temperatures, talking to the people who were willing to talk, checking in on the folks—just in case—who told us, night after night, to go away, I repeated a different phrase to myself. A slight variation of Bradford, and, I believe, more accurate: "Here, for the grace of God, we go."

We went, because that was where the grace of God lived: under this bridge, on this park bench, in this alcove. God lived in those homes we call home-less. "Foxes have dens," Jesus once said, "and the birds in the sky have nests, but the Human One has no place to lay his head" (Matthew 8:20, *CEB*). It was not the grace of God that separated me from the experience of those sleeping outside. It was the grace of God that connected me to them. And so, I prayed as we walked and talked. Prayed for this grace to be felt. To be seen and heard. To somehow become more concrete than the concrete on which some slept on those cold, cold nights.

There go I. For—not by—the grace of God.

Institutions, Care, and Better Conversations

Walking around those Georgetown neighborhoods, I thought back to the psychologist who told me that most men with my diagnosis end up in jail. Chronic homelessness and mass incarceration have replaced a functioning mental health system for far too many people in this country. That reality is often linked to the history of deinstitutionalization in this country. But do we need more mental healthcare institutions? Are more psychiatric beds the answer?

These questions often reenter the national discourse after mass shootings, a toxic association which we have already unpacked. But the discussion around institutionalization is close to my heart. My own story, and my experiences with psychiatric hospitalization, are the starting point for both my writing and my advocacy. As I have said before, my story is just one story, and there is more to be said about institutionalization than my experience on "the psych ward," which, though one of the most painful and difficult times of my life, was nevertheless characterized overall by safety and healing, however gradual.

My experience was a privileged one. I had access to quality care and to people who knew how to connect me to quality care, which are not realities that can be taken for granted by most people in the United States. I also had a level of awareness of my own need for help, both because of conversations within my family about mental illness and also because of the nature of my illness. My racial identity and socioeconomic background, among other factors, allowed me a level of access that is often denied to people who are impacted by multiple oppressions. Yet, in spite of all of my advantages, psychiatric hospitalization felt scary, isolating, and out of my control. I am very grateful for the hospitals that kept me safe and gave me space to stabilize and start on the path toward healing, and I realize that conversations around psychiatric hospitalization, and even more so long-term institutionalization, require a great deal of care, compassion, and nuance.

My time in and out of psychiatric hospitalization looked nothing like the popular perception of it, which in my own pre-hospitalization experience was a mishmash of *One Flew Over the Cuckoo's Nest*–esque images of straitjackets and dictatorial nurses. Suffice to say it's important that we destigmatize psychiatric hospitalization. It saved my life. At the same time, we need to acknowledge the history of institutional abuse and neglect and be careful that our approach to mental healthcare institutions is focused on compassionate and effective care. Reactionary, stigmatizing rhetoric does not help.

Deinstitutionalization began in the 1960s and 1970s as a response to civil rights and mental health advocates who spoke out against institutional abuse and neglect. The idea was to close big institutions, which were horrendous and often served not so much as healthcare centers as prisons for folks who didn't "fit," and replace them with community mental health centers that would be smaller, more localized, and more integrated into communities, allowing for people with mental illnesses to remain connected to other sources of support like families, faith communities, friends, and other community services.

During the 1980s, community mental health centers fell victim to tax cuts and lack of funding. Rather than transitioning from big, awful institutions to smaller, community-based centers, we moved from institutions to not much of anything at all, or from prison-like institutions to plain old prisons. The political forces that pushed for cuts failed to consider the true cost of their decisions. Many advocates trace the modern realities of homelessness to the decisions made during this period.

Currently, there is a massive shortage of psychiatric beds in this country. According to a report by the D.C.-based Treatment Advocacy Center with the biblically resonant title "No Room At The Inn," in 2010 there were only about fourteen beds available for every 100 thousand people.[2] This shortage, among other factors, means that hospital emergency rooms, prisons, and shelters have effectively taken the place of psychiatric hospitalization for many people experiencing serious mental illness. Like everything else in this country, the reality is further impacted by racial and socioeconomic factors. Who gets a bed and who ends up in prison are affected by intersecting and oppressive systems.

We need more psychiatric beds. When I give talks in congregations, particularly in more rural areas of the country, I will often hear that communities have a complete lack of dedicated hospital care for mental health or substance abuse crises. This is a huge and potentially deadly gap in vital services. But that does not make institutions the be-all and end-all of mental healthcare, nor can we ignore vital criticisms of the abuses of institutions. Institutions create power imbalances that can lead to abuse when patients are seen as objects of control rather than subjects in need of care.

We need more and better mental healthcare facilities, but the rhetoric on the matter is often stigmatizing, reactionary, and harmful.

---

2. Treatment Advocacy Center, "No Room at the Inn: Trends and Consequences of Closing Public Psychiatric Hospitals, 2005–2010," Report, July 19, 2012, available online: *https://www.treatmentadvocacycenter.org/storage/documents/no_room_at_the_inn-2012.pdf.*

It ought to go without saying, but of course it doesn't these days, that to say we need more institutions to deal with "sickos" and "insane monsters" demonizes and scapegoats people with mental illnesses.[3] We need more and better care options for folks with mental illness because folks with mental illness are people who deserve care, compassion, and health.

Psychiatric hospitalization saved my life.

We need more—and better—mental healthcare facilities. We don't have them. The importance of these institutions deserves a conversation focused on compassion, care, and effective treatment, not a reactionary conversation blaming people with mental illnesses.

Prison Isn't Good for Your Health

We can't talk about "bringing institutions back" without acknowledging that the prison system is standing in for an actual mental care system in this country. The National Alliance on Mental Illness (NAMI) summarizes the crisis:

> In a mental health crisis, people are more likely to encounter police than get medical help. As a result, 2 million people with mental illness are booked into jails each year. Nearly 15% of men and 30% of women booked into jails have a serious mental health condition. . . . Once in jail, many individuals don't receive the treatment they need and end up getting worse, not better. . . . After leaving jail, many no longer have access to needed healthcare and benefits. A criminal record often makes it hard for individuals to get a job or housing. Many individuals, especially without access to mental health services and supports, wind up homeless, in emergency rooms and often re-arrested.[4]

---

3. Alison Kodjak, "Experts Say There's Little Connection between Mental Health and Mass Shootings," *All Things Considered*, February 23, 2018, available online: *https://www.npr.org/2019/04/10/711714596/colorados-red-flag-gun-measure-raises-concerns.*

4. National Alliance on Mental Illness, "Jailing People with Mental Illness," available online: *https://www.nami.org/learn-more/public-policy/jailing-people-with-mental-illness.*

According to journalist Alisa Roth, the three largest psychiatric institutions in the country are all prisons: New York's Rikers Island, Chicago's Cook County Jail, and the Los Angeles County Jail. Prisons act as revolving doors in more than one way, with many people cycling in between incarceration, mental healthcare in the community, and homelessness.[5] I've witnessed that cycle personally. One of my fellow patients in D.C. was released from the hospital only to return to an insecure housing situation—hardly a recipe for successful recovery. On the streets of Georgetown, we spoke regularly to a gentleman, previously incarcerated, who had then been diverted to a public psychiatric hospital and whose official release papers from that hospital indicated that the home to which he was being released was a local park bench.

The revolving door back into incarceration isn't even the worst possible outcome of an encounter with law enforcement, as the "risk of being killed while being approached or stopped by law enforcement in the community is sixteen times higher for individuals with untreated serious mental illness than for other civilians" and "at least one in four fatal law enforcement encounters involves an individual with serious mental illness."[6] In just one example, police in New York shot and killed Saheed Vassell, a Jamaican immigrant who suffered from bipolar disorder and was well known by his community, after they encountered him holding what turned out to be a showerhead.[7] Our system is horrifically broken. The consequences of it are deadly.

Multiple systems interact and impact each other simultaneously. Systemic racism, economic injustice, the for-profit prison industry,

5. Interview with Alisa Roth by Ailsa Chang, "'Insane: America's 3 Largest Psychiatric Facilities Are Jails," *All Things Considered*, April 25, 2018, available online: *https://www.npr.org/sections/health-shots/2018/04/25/605666107/insane-americas-3-largest-psychiatric-facilities-are-jails*.

6. "Overlooked in the Undercounted: The Role of Mental Illness in Fatal Law Enforcement Encounters," *Treatment Advocacy Center*, December 2015, available online: *https://www.treatmentadvocacycenter.org/overlooked-in-the-undercounted*.

7. "Headline: New York Police Kill Bipolar Jamaican Immigrant Holding Object That Looked Like Shower Head," *Democracy Now*, April 5, 2018, available online: *https://www.democracynow.org/2018/4/5/headlines/nypd_shoot_dead_bipolar_jamaican_immigrant_holding_object_that_looked_like_shower_head*.

and educational inequities, among other forces, interact to intensify the crisis of mass incarceration replacing a functional mental health-care system. Civil rights lawyer Michelle Alexander has referred to the intersection of racism and mass incarceration as "the New Jim Crow,"[8] while Marian Wright Edelman of the Children's Defense Fund refers to the "cradle to prison pipeline" that leaves economically disadvantaged children of color vulnerable to incarceration, a situation exacerbated by disparities in mental healthcare.

> The lack of health and mental healthcare among low-income children is also an important factor in a child's educational development. A child's misbehavior may be a reflection of an unaddressed learning disability or mental or emotional disorder. Regrettably, too few schools have the staff capable of recognizing the behavior of a disturbed or disabled child for what it is, and if they do, are unable to provide treatment. More often, these children are seen as "disruptive," and instead of offering them counseling or psychological therapy, too many educators dispense "zero tolerance" discipline—usually in the form of suspensions or expulsions.[9]

The labeling of children of color as "disruptive" is related to the historical use of pseudo-psychology as a tool of oppression.

In the mid-1800s, two supposed psychological "diagnoses" were given to enslaved African Americans who resisted their oppressive condition:

> *Drapetomania* was characterized by a single symptom, the uncontrollable urge to escape slavery. *Dysaesthesia aethiopis* was the diagnosis recommended for any of the following symptoms: destroying property on the plantation, being disobedient, talking back, fighting with masters, or refusing to work. In both of these

---

8. Michelle Alexander, *The New Jim Crow: Mass Incarceration in the Age of Colorblindness* (The New Press, 2012); see also *http://newjimcrow.com/about.*

9. Marian Wright Edelman, "From School Yard to Prison Yard," *Child Watch Column*, November 2, 2007, available online: *https://www.childrensdefense.org/child-watch-columns/health/2007/from-school-yard-to-prison-yard/.*

"conditions," the system of chattel slavery as a precipitating factor was rendered invisible.[10]

While these particular "diagnoses" have long since been debunked, the ghost of this sort of social and psychological malpractice continues to haunt contemporary diagnoses when "socially constructed 'insanities' are eliminated and those whose behaviors risk compromising the social order are silenced."[11] For example, African Americans are routinely misdiagnosed with more severe mental health issues than white patients with the same presenting symptoms.[12] This history adds intensified layers of stigma to mental healthcare in the communities that have inherited this trauma.

Means of Control or Means of Grace?

Modern psychological models can function as "sites of control" rather than as agents of healing.[13] The tendency for the language of care to be subverted into language of control leads me to reflect on the way I understand mental healthcare in general and medication in particular. In *Christ on the Psych Ward,* I wrote about learning to make theological meaning out of taking medication: "I thought of my glass of water and handful of pills as a strange sort of sacrament, an outward and visible sign of the inward and invisible work of healing, somehow making present in limited materiality the unlimited activity of God."[14] Medication, for me, has been a means of grace. Though we do not work to earn God's grace or favor, there are tangible things, be they practices or materials in our life, through which grace is somehow

---

10. Cedric C. Johnson, *Race, Religion, and Resilience in the Neoliberal Age* (New York: Palgrave Macmillan, 2016), 4.

11. Johnson, *Race, Religion, and Resilience*, 4.

12. Patti Verbanas, "African-Americans more likely to be misdiagnosed with schizophrenia, study finds," *ScienceDaily*, March 21, 2019, available online: *https://www.sciencedaily.com/releases/2019/03/190321130300.htm.*

13. Johnson, *Race, Religion, and Resilience,* 4.

14. David Finnegan-Hosey, *Christ on the Psych Ward* (New York: Church Publishing, 2018), 136.

communicated to us, and through which we can put ourselves in the way of grace. The sacraments of baptism and communion are examples of means of grace, of course, though not the only ones.

The phrase "outward and visible sign of an inward invisible grace" has been used to describe the sacraments at least since Augustine, and I have come to understand medication, and mental health treatment in general, as a tangible, outward sign of God's grace which is calling all of us into health and wholeness and healing. This, for me, has provided a depth of meaning and a spiritual narrative around medication that the purely medical model has often been unable to provide for people, which has sometimes made the medical model feel alienating and isolating for people like me for whom spirituality is important.

Even as I began to articulate the idea of medication as a means of grace, I simultaneously gained a better understanding of how medication can be used as a means of control. In the summer of 2018, as I was driving up and down the East Coast sharing about my experiences and working to destigmatize conversations about medication and mental healthcare in faith communities, news broke that powerful psychotropic medications were being forcibly administered to children who had been separated from their families while attempting to cross the U.S.-Mexico border and were being held in cages.[15]

In an unrelated case, the Missouri foster care system has faced lawsuits over its use of antipsychotic drugs on children as young as toddlers.[16] Beyond these forms of unjust, even criminal, malpractice,

---

15. Christina Zhao, "Migrant Children Separated From Parents at Border Were Forcibly Drugged: Lawsuit," *Newsweek*, June 21, 2018, available online: *https://www. newsweek.com/migrant-children-separated-parents-border-were-forced-take-drugs-lawsuit-988069*; Aura Bogado, "Doctor giving migrant kids psychotropic drugs lost certification years ago," *The Texas Tribune,* June 26, 2018, *https://www.texastribune. org/2018/06/26/doctor-giving-migrant-kids-psychotropic-drugs-lost-certification-years/*.

16. Robert Patrick, "Missouri overuses psychotropic drugs on foster children, federal suit claims," *St. Louis Post-Dispatch,* June 12, 2017, available online: *https://www. stltoday.com/news/local/crime-and-courts/missouri-overuses-psychotropic-drugs-on-foster-children-federal-suit-claims/article_27e27c66-6e60-56ba-9cc2-9de8488358b8. html*; Dan Margolies, "Case Over Psychotropic Drugs Given to Missouri Foster Kids Now Class-Action Lawsuit," *KCUR.org,* available online: *https://www.kcur.org/post/ case-over-psychotropic-drugs-given-missouri-foster-kids-now-class-action-lawsuit#stream/0*.

many people have experiences of medications and institutions that are traumatic, alienating, and heavily associated with a lack of autonomy. Mary Button, artist, theologian, and creator of *Stations of the Cross: Mental Illness*, shared at the Wild Goose Festival about her own experiences with hospitalization:

> Having a mental illness doesn't mean that you no longer have the right to bodily autonomy. . . . That's just the truth. . . . When I was hospitalized, I saw very powerful drugs being used as chemical restraints, that a patient's behavior was disruptive and so they would be shot up with Haldol or put into restraints and to me I think that deepens the trauma, and it's a type of violence, and it's a type of violence that's perpetrated by the medical community.[17]

Even as medications can be used as a means of control, 83 percent of those incarcerated while having a mental illness do not have access to proper treatment.[18] The Rev. Kayla Bonewell, a United Church of Christ pastor in Oklahoma City who assisted an incarcerated parishioner to start an LGBTQ-affirming prison ministry, shares about the provision of powerful antipsychotic drugs coupled with the lack of holistic treatment in the prison setting:

> When we were leaving [the prison] last Thursday, there was this long line of mostly men who were waiting outside . . . the hospital building, and I was told that that is the pill line, so that is everyone who . . . have mental health diagnoses, and it's like antipsychotic medication, because that's all that is done. There's not the counseling, there's not the other things that people get to have for health.[19]

---

17. Mary Button, interview by Marthame Sanders, "Mental Health, Theology, and Creativity—David Finnegan-Hosey & Mary Button," *Wild Goose Festival*, July 14, 2018, available online: *www.youtube.com/watch?v=eJ20wEwKAUs or http://wild goosefestival.org/experience/*.

18. National Alliance on Mental Illness, "Jailing People with Mental Illness," available online: *https://www.nami.org/learn-more/public-policy/jailing-people-with-mental-illness*.

19. Interview with Kayla Bonewell by Sarah Elizabeth Smith, "Episode 21: Open & Affirming Prison Ministry with the Rev. Kayla Bonewell," *The Theosophia Podcast*, July 9, 2019, available online: *https://www.theosophiapodcast.com/about-1*.

In the absence of a comprehensive approach to care, medication serves, not as a source of healing, but a site of control. This is emphasized by the medical language used to describe those who take or do not take their prescribed medication: "compliant" and "non-compliant," respectively. A system where compliance is always good and non-compliance bad is a system with a deep-seated need for control.

The use of instruments of care as instruments of power is worthy of ethical challenge and condemnation in its own right. It also impacts the important conversation around destigmatizing medication and mental health treatment in general. It is much more difficult to destigmatize psychiatric care and medication when the treatment is associated with trauma. It is harder to convince people that psychiatric wards are not *One Flew Over the Cuckoo's Nest* when drugs are used as restraints and incarceration has replaced and replicated the past abuses of mental health institutions. It is hard to have the crucial conversation about more psychiatric beds and more options for care when the means of care are experienced by many as means of control. The challenge and the calling of the faith community is to hold all of these at times contradicting concerns in a space of compassion and care so we can heal sick systems and work together as a society toward health and wholeness.

The Vocation of Healing in a World of Works-Based Value

Walking around the streets of Washington, D.C., or any other city, on the coldest nights of the year offers an eyewitness encounter with the brutal ways our systems fail people, discard people, and ignore the fundamental worth of people who are *imago Dei*, made in the image of God. God has not abandoned people. We have. And one of the ways we have abandoned each other is by placing our fundamental valuing of each other in the wrong place—in our ability to produce or achieve rather than our basic, divinely created humanity.

> [Within] present day capitalist societies, where work is viewed as fundamental to popular understandings of worthwhile human

> existence, a person's employment is a major source of value, self-worth, and economic sustenance. . . . This exclusion from primary sources of value leaves many people with [mental health challenges] feeling there is no future for them. Consequently, life appears profoundly hopeless and meaningless.[20]

For people caught in the revolving door of mental illness, homelessness, and incarceration, the systemic devaluing of their existence in a society that values those who are perceived as independent and productive wears down their very ability to participate in that society in an escalating spiral.

This phenomenon is not limited only to those with mental health struggles. Church historian Justo González tells the story of visiting a congregation composed mostly of poor day laborers and their families. The preacher asked the congregants to indicate by show of hands how many days they had been able to find work in the previous week. One day? Two? Three? The higher the number, the fewer hands were raised. The preacher concluded, "How, then, are we to obey the law of God that commands that we shall work six days when we cannot even find work for a single day?"[21] Contrast this story with the experience many in our capitalist society have of being overworked, overcommitted, and burned out. These two seemingly opposite interactions are in fact two sides of the same coin: some overworked to exhaustion, while others are denied opportunities for meaningful work.

My experience of bipolar disorder has at times been a spinning coin, pushing myself to the point of burnout at times, often with the unconscious motivation of trying to prove my own worth and ability, and unable to work with all of the attendant doubting of my own value at other times. I recently commented to my wife that it feels as if my manic brain is constantly making commitments that my depressed brain can't follow through on. If only I could switch the two! But the

---

20. John Swinton, *Resurrecting the Person: Friendship and the Care of People with Mental Health Problems* (Nashville: Abingdon Press, 2000), 93.

21. Justo L. González, *Santa Biblia: The Bible through Hispanic Eyes* (Nashville: Abingdon, 1996), 59–60.

reality of my conundrum is not just a function of my brain, it is a way in which my diagnosed mental illness has interacted with the systemic nature of our economic system and its hidden ranking of value and ability, all of which run counter to the notion of finding our identity in our divine createdness.

Traditional Christian concepts of vocation have often bought into this same problematic framework, however inadvertently associating the idea of calling with the ability to find and keep gainful employment. This association can be understood as an unintended consequence of the otherwise laudable insistence of the Protestant Reformers, particularly Luther, that vocation was not a special category only applicable to those called to be professional holy people, priests and religious, but a calling on the life of all Christians.

Centuries later, we sometimes substitute the word "vocation" in modern English with the word "trade," as in "vocational schools"; alternatively, we contrast it with the concept of "avocation," something one feels passionate about but does not get paid to do.

This definition of vocation is, if you'll excuse the pun, an impoverished one. From a Christian theological perspective, vocation is grounded first and foremost not in our *activity* but in our *identity* as children of God and as participants in *God's* gracious activity in the world, which is not dependent on our ability to find gainful employment or advance ourselves in a capitalist economic system. Our participation is possible, first and foremost, not because of our abilities but because of the gift of God's grace.

I am not suggesting that vocation has nothing to do with material considerations, but that God's calling operates at a deeper, a more basic level than is recognized or valued by the economic system of capitalism. Patrick B. Reyes writes of first recognizing his vocation, not in the halls of higher education or in a mountaintop moment, but in a traumatic experience of violence from his childhood when he was slammed up against the wall by his mother's abusive boyfriend.

> In this moment, all I wanted to do was live. [Vocation] is about living. It is about hearing God's call in the moment when we are

suspended, off the ground, the moment when we have no way of knowing how or when we will get down or whether we will still be breathing when we do. It is about discerning the call to life in the midst of almost certain death.[22]

Reyes speaks of vocation in terms of a calling to life, a calling to survive. For those experiencing violence and oppression, this deep call to survival is a participation in God's desire for abundant life for God's creation. Vocation is first and foremost responding to that call, and to nurture that call to life in others.

To say that vocation is about something deeper, more basic, than someone's ability to pay their own way is not to say that vocation is disconnected from material needs. Vocation is about breathing, about survival, about the very stuff of life. But a calling to life is experienced by all of God's children, whether or not their ability, or access to care, or experience in an unjust economic system affords them the opportunity of a steady job. A calling to life is not just about the individual but about caring for the community and working for the common good.

We are called. All of us. Called. Called into health and wholeness. Called to life. Called to the image of God that we can only find in each other. Called to go to those places—yes, *those* places—for that is where the grace of God resides.

---

22. Patrick B. Reyes, *Nobody Cries When We Die: God, Community, and Surviving to Adulthood* (St. Louis, MO: Chalice Press, 2016), 11–12.

PART

3

Care

We are saved *by* pre-existing grace,
from unhealthy systems,
for the common good.

"For we are what God has made us, created in Christ Jesus for good works, which God prepared beforehand to be our way of life" (Ephesians 2:10). We are created in and through the pre-existing Christ in an act which is pure grace, pure gift. But it is a gift with a purpose: to foment good works, actions that manifest the same grace and care with which we are created. Rather than establishing a dichotomy between God's activity and human action, the writer of Ephesians understands grace and good works as intrinsically connected. If grace is the true pre-existing condition of creation, then good works are how humans participate in the coming-into-fruition of God's initial creative purpose.

What's more, good works, just like grace, are not to be understood individualistically. In the verses immediately following the one above, the letter writer speaks of the way in which Christ brings together those who had previously been divided—in the case of the church at Ephesus, Jewish and Gentile believers. The passage not only describes the way in which grace enables the shared life of the church but also speaks of the breaking down of divisions within the church, which in this letter is not "the local congregations to which Paul refers but the universal—even cosmic—reality of the one church (2:16).[1]

---

1. E. Elizabeth Johnson, "Ephesians," in *Women's Bible Commentary: Revised and Updated,* 3rd ed., ed. Carol A. Newsom, Sharon H. Ringe, and Jacqueline E. Lapsley (Louisville: Westminster John Knox, 2012), 577.

Mitzi J. Smith draws a comparison between the "dividing wall" or "barrier of separation" that the author claims Jesus has overcome, and the segregation experienced by African Americans in the modern era: "African Americans are all too familiar with 'barriers of separation' that historically and currently attempt to limit our full participation as U.S. citizens."[2] We will not have to reach far to come up with other examples of dividing walls, enforced by societal prejudice, political realities, and systems of power, experienced by people whom Christ calls to be gathered into one community. God's plan for all of the cosmos, according to Ephesians, is "to gather up all things in Christ, things in heaven and things on earth" (Ephesians 1:10). The good works we have been created for take place in the context of God's work to bring all of creation back together in the heart of God.

---

2. Mitzi J. Smith, "Ephesians," in *True to Our Native Land: An African American New Testament Commentary*, ed. Brian K. Blount et al. (Minneapolis: Fortress, 2007), 353.

6

Care, Context, and the Common Good

We live in overwhelming times, and my mind is easily overwhelmed even on my best of days. I'm increasingly convinced of the need to expand the conversation around mental healthcare so that we are not only challenging stigma and breaking silence but also confronting unjust and broken systems. I'm simultaneously aware of how overwhelming it is to feel trapped in a web of invisible powers and interlocking systems. Many people right now have much to feel anxious about. Whole communities are being scapegoated and denigrated at the highest level of public life. Relief workers and trauma-care providers and faith leaders are responding to drastic human need. And then there's me. Sometimes I'm anxious because my brain decided to be anxious this week.

This is, to put it lightly, annoying. It's just part of my experience of living with mental illness, and though I have lots of supports in place, it also sucks. Recently, while journaling, I happened on a favorite passage in one of Paul's letters to the church in Corinth: "To each is given the manifestation of the Spirit for the common good" (1 Corinthians 12:7). The verse is part of Paul's exploration of spiritual gifts, or *charismaton*—a word directly related to the Greek words for grace and gratitude. The manifestations of the Spirit for the common good are gifts of God's grace. I scribbled, "What do I say to my brain when it tells me I'm a drain on the common good? What does the Spirit say to me when my brain is telling me I'm a drain on the common good?"

That's a pretty good summary of what my brain does when it's in an anxiety spiral. It tells me I'm a drain on the common good. I know that is not true. I know mental illness lies to me. But my brain can be awfully convincing. What I would love to be able to do is just ignore the voice of anxiety, ignore the voice of depression, ignore the voice of bipolar disorder. But when I try to stuff it down and move on and get back to working for the common good, that voice figures out how to infiltrate my efforts and comes back louder and stronger. I often find myself asking this question: how do I care about the world when my brain feels like a dumpster fire?

Thinking about systems can seem overwhelming. And yet, thinking systems—and understanding self-care, not as an individualistic act, but as an act that happens in community, that is, within a system—provides a key to easing the anxiety created by the complexities of the systems that harm us.[1]

Everything happens in the context of systems: family systems, congregational systems, macro-systems. Something that happens in one part of a system affects the other parts. None of us is an atomized unit. For better and for worse, we are inextricably connected to our families, our contexts, our communities. At the same time, while everything happens in systems, no individual is completely identifiable with a particular system. I am deeply affected by my family, by my community, and by my participation in systems of race and gender. But I am not my family. I am not my gender. I am a complex person in a complex context. Being able to remember that "I am me" in the midst of all the systems that affect me is referred to as "self-differentiation."

A system affects the individuals within it; conversely, individuals within a system can affect it. If my family system is in chaos, that affects me. And my actions or level of anxiety can amplify or absorb some of the chaos in my family. Intervention in one part or one level of a system affects the other parts. This means when we are thinking about an intervention—be it a counseling session, an educational program, or an organizing strategy—we have to do two things simultaneously:

---

1. I owe much of my understanding of family systems theory and its interpretation in macro-contexts to Dr. Cedric C. Johnson's "PC-111: Pastoral Care and Counseling in Contexts" at Wesley Theological Seminary, in which I learned as a student and then as his TA for two semesters.

keep the whole system in mind, and not allow the complexity of the system to paralyze us.

Take, for example, an individual who seeks counseling. Many traditional counseling approaches focus entirely on that individual, and, in particular, on any pathology shown by that individual, rather than considering their family system or the effects of macro-systems like race, class, or economics. This isn't particularly effective. At the same time, no single counseling session, or even series of counseling sessions, can move every part of every system that affects the individual. We have to pick a place to start, given our understanding of the context in which the individual is operating.

The language of family systems theory largely originates from Dr. Murray Bowen, who was interested in the ways in which we all become emotionally interlocked with other members of our family and in the generational patterns that tend to occur in families.[2] But systems theory has been applied to all sorts of other areas, including congregational life and contemplative prayer.[3] Rabbi Edwin Friedman related systems theory to leadership.[4] The key concept from his work is "self-differentiation." The idea is that the best thing one can do for a system is to self-differentiate: to have good boundaries, avoid being sucked into other people's anxiety, and maintain a non-anxious presence.

A few caveats are worth mentioning. Self-differentiation is different from individualism. Self-differentiation *assumes* a systems perspective. That is, it assumes we are all in systems, all interdependent; that's the context in which self-differentiation is important.

---

2. See the website of the Bowen Center for the Study of the Family at *http://the bowencenter.org/theory/murray-bowen/*.

3. See Ronald W. Richardson, *Creating a Healthier Church* (Augsburg Fortress, 2006); Peter Scazzaro, *The Emotionally Healthy Church* (Zondervan, 2015); and Paul David Lawson, *Old Wine in New Skins: Centering Prayer and Systems Theory* (Lantern Books, 2000).

4. See Edwin Friedman, *A Failure of Nerve: Leadership in the Age of the Quick Fix* (New York: Seabury, 2007); for a brief summary of Friedman's work, see Dr. Jonathan Camp, "Friedman's Theory of Differentiated Leadership Made Simple," November 10, 2010, available online: *https://www.youtube.com/watch?v=RgdcljNV-Ew*.

Self-differentiation is thus not the opposite of empathy, but the ability to hold the tension between the necessity of empathy and connection and the temptation to get sucked into the anxiety of my family/workplace/congregation/society. Good boundaries and good empathy are mutually reinforcing, not contradictory.[5]

"Non-anxious" and "self-differentiated" do not necessarily mean "calm, cool, and collected." Sometimes, leading and organizing mean turning up the level of anxiety to make change happen. Non-anxious presence is about being able to manage the anxiety that is always present in systems. Why is all this important? Because one of the best things we can do to positively affect systems is to take good care of ourselves.

On Feeling Whelmed, Over and Otherwise

If you're feeling overwhelmed in this present moment, you are not alone. Many people are feeling like you do. In truth, it's no accident. Oppressive systems are designed to make people feel overwhelmed. Avoiding being overwhelmed—or, at least, being able to "ride the whelming wave"—is vital right now. A systems approach can help us resist, ride out, or differentiate within, the systems marked by intentionally created anxiety. Systems theory reminds us that there are big systems that impact us, and that those systems are tough, though not impossible, to change.

It's not just you. You are not alone. Change is hard work that requires a certain resilience for the long haul. That resilience happens in community, with others who are also working for change and also feeling overwhelmed. It's not just you. You are not alone. And you don't have to do everything. No one person, or even one community, can do everything. That's okay. Remember as long as we keep an eye on the systems at play, an intervention at one level of the system can affect the whole thing. So, you can acknowledge the systems at play and pick one thing to focus on.

---

5. Brené Brown, *Rising Strong* (New York: Spiegel & Grau, 2015), 99ff.

Remember that self-care positively affects the system. By caring for yourself and your health and well-being, you help make the system healthier. I don't mean that we can just care for ourselves and forget about the rest of the system. I mean self-care is a deeply contextual act; self-care doesn't have to be another individualistic goal to be achieved. In systems theory, self-care happens in context. It includes checking on each other, supporting each other, encouraging each other, loving each other. Call it "self-care-in-context," or "self-care-in-community." Some need to step back from speaking out or marching; for others, speaking out will most benefit their self-understanding and mental health; for most of us, both are true, depending on what else is happening in our lives.

Internal work and external work go hand-in-hand. Self-care does not equal isolation. "Self-differentiation" is internal work in systems theory language, but we can also name it as prayer, meditation, counseling, contemplation—all of it makes our external work more effective. External work—marching, educating, organizing, writing, caring for others—can reinforce our internal work rather than "taking away" from it, and vice versa. "Self-care" isn't an excuse to isolate or give up. It's part of our overall work, just as caring for each other is part of how we care for ourselves.

Anxiety can't be eliminated, but it can be borne. Christ "bears along," according to Hebrews 1:3, and we who follow Christ are called to bear along as well. Systems theory uses the terminology of "anxiety" to refer to the tension or disturbances within a system. Anxiety never goes away; what systems theory points to is how we learn to manage, handle, or ride out anxiety. In dialectical behavior therapy, which I was introduced to in the hospital, there's a technique called "riding the wave" that I've found helpful. When you're feeling overwhelmed (a word that literally refers to being engulfed or submerged, as by a wave) you don't necessarily have to fight that feeling. Acknowledge that it's there, and that it might bowl you over for a bit. But also know that this particular wave will subside, and you will be able to right yourself and keep moving. Another wave will come, and it will hit you hard too, but you can learn to ride each wave instead of feeling drowned by them.

In our current social and political crisis, it's important to keep in mind that whole systems need to change. No single thing is going to be the one thing that does it. We need to acknowledge that and try not to get defensive about it. The one or three things that I can focus on today—the protest I can attend, the representative I can call—isn't going to fix everything. We can't all move everything at once. Care for yourself and for others, knowing that the struggle is both urgent and long-term. Pick a place you think you can intervene. Do it, knowing that your actions are part of a larger system.

Care, Systems, and the Trinity

Speaking about care in the context of systems opens a doorway into the mystery that is the Triune God. The doctrine of the Trinity is one of those seemingly esoteric theological concepts that can be perceived as the domain of out-of-touch dogmatists. In fairness, the admittedly strange idea of a God who is One In Three, Three In One has tripped up more than a few theological heavyweights. None other than Barton Warren Stone, one of the founders of the movement that would become my Disciples of Christ denomination, almost failed his ordination exams because he couldn't bring himself to accept every aspect of the church's accumulated teaching about the Trinity.

In his book *Narratives of a Vulnerable God*, theologian William C. Placher notes how strange it seemed to him to spend time exploring what some saw as an obscure and irrelevant idea. But, he writes, "if we Christians understand the doctrine of the Trinity aright, we will realize that it implies that God is not about power and self-sufficiency and the assertion of authority but about mutuality and equality and love.[6] Like Placher, I have come to believe that there is something important about the Christian theological imagination of a God described in terms of relationship and unity-in-community.

The Trinity is a relationship of three persons who are, at the same time, unified and differentiated. We who are made in the image of that

---

6. William C. Placher, *Narratives of a Vulnerable God: Christ, Theology, and Scripture* (Louisville, KY: Westminster John Knox, 1994), 53–55.

God, then, must be understood in terms of relationships that overcome alienation and brokenness and lead to mutual uplift and wholeness. At the same time, to speak of humans made in the image of God as fundamentally connected and unified is not to suggest that we all collapse together into one big, enmeshed blob. God is One, but God is not a monolith, and neither are we called to be.

We are called, rather, to live into the image of God in which we were created. That means caring for ourselves without isolating ourselves, accepting care from others while maintaining our sense of self, caring for others without entirely losing our unique identities. It means, too, imagining and then acting for a world in which our communities and the systems that impact our neighbors and us might reflect the reality of their creator, who is perfection in mutual love. God as Trinity stands in contrast with a world marked by competition, domination, and violence. To witness to the Triune God triumphant over the powers of evil in the world—the God who by the power of the Spirit "raised Christ from the dead and seated him at God's right hand in the heavenly places, far above all rule and authority and power and dominion" and has "put all things under Christ's feet" (Ephesians 1:20–22)—is to imagine a world in which a healthy system of mutual love, hospitality, and uplift has replaced the unhealthy system of brokenness, fragmentation, oppression, and harm.

What's more, acting in light of this Triune unity-in-community isn't a ceaseless striving after unreachable perfection, as if by individual willpower we can try harder to be like God. Rather, we are actively invited into the reality of the Trinity, our limited humanity welcomed and included and made full by the transforming love of God. The same God who has "put all things under Christ's feet" has also "made Christ the head over all things for the church, which is his body, the fullness of him who fills all in all" (Ephesians 1:22–23) and has "made us alive together with Christ—by grace you have been saved—and raised us up with him and seated us with him in the heavenly places in Christ Jesus" (Ephesians 2:5–6).

God is relational in and of God's self and welcomes us into that relationality. God's gracious salvation is an invitation to participate in the mutual love of the Trinity. According to Jurgen Moltmann, "the unity of the triune God is an inviting and uniting unity, and as such a unity which is open to human beings and the world."[7] Humans are invited into the Trinity's community. We are invited to leave behind alienation and fear and experience God's welcome. We are invited to participate in the divine indwelling. We are invited to not be alone. We are invited by a God who is "rich in mercy . . . out of the great love with which God has loved us" (Ephesians 2:4).

Personal experience of God is communal experience as well. The church's call to reflect the Triune nature of God has implications for how we understand Christian community, which in turn has implications for how we come to experience God. And it has implications for how we care for each other and ourselves, how we act for the common good. When we, the church, the Body of Christ, are sent out into the world, we are not sent out as invulnerable automatons or invincible warriors, but as reflections of the love of God who, even in God's self, expresses mutual care and compassion. The Trinity holds love in common within God's self, reminding us through love that we, too, are part of the common good.

Being Enough, Not Doing Enough

Part of learning how to care for myself and others in the midst of the complexity of systems has been figuring out how to navigate the sense that I am not doing enough without falling into the trap of thinking that I'm not enough. It is important for me to keep that simple fact about my emotional life and my mental health in view. When I don't, bad things happen. Breakdown things. Hospital things. Avoiding those things, and all the practices and habits that avoidance entails, including visits with my counselor and my psychiatrist, must be a priority for me. The thing I need to keep in view is the simple emotional fact that "I'm just not doing enough" can be a toxic message for me. By "toxic," I don't mean, "bums me out." I mean, "sends me into harmful

---

7. Jurgen Moltmann, *History and the Triune God: Contributions to Trinitarian Theology* (New York: Crossroad, 1992), 87.

spirals of self-hate and potentially even self-harm." I mean, "is bad not only for the intangible contours of my emotional, mental, spiritual health but for my concrete physical health."

It could be argued that such a consideration is a privilege, and indeed, as with many aspects of my life, privilege plays a role. But ignoring such things is a privilege in and of itself. Only within the remarkable privilege of the post-industrial "West" does the insistence that "doing more" is always the best way forward cohere. It is the privileged few rather than the oppressed many that tend toward "functional atheism," a term defined by Parker Palmer as "the unconscious, unexamined conviction that if anything decent is going to happen here, we are the ones who must make it happen—a conviction held even by people who talk a good game about God."[8]

Oppression and violence are, of course, also bad for the physical, emotional, mental, and spiritual health of their victims and need to be opposed for many reasons. But I am conscious of living in a tension between the very real sense that I am not doing enough to confront racism, or sexism, or heterosexism, or violence, or mendacity, or oppression and the reality that this sense is harmful, not only to myself but to those around me.

Tension is a word I use often, and it's one whose meaning is easy to lose sight of. Think of a rubber band, which only does its work by holding tension between two poles. If the band is pulled too much, it breaks, but if it is not pulled at all, it serves no function, no purpose. The purpose is in the tension.

Here is the relevant tension, the two poles that must be pulled against each other if any work is to be done, if anything is to be held together: It is true that I am not doing enough. This is true because of the simple fact that, short of Jesus coming back, there will never be a time when enough has been done, when the work is finished, the struggle won. It is also true that I am enough because I am, and you are, made in the divine image, breathed into being by the Spirit, loved madly and wildly by a God who creates in and through love. If I only

8. Parker Palmer, *Let Your Life Speak: Listening for the Voice of Vocation* (John Wiley & Sons, 2000), 88.

look to "I am not doing enough," then more than burnout happens to me. Personal collapse happens to me. My actions and activity come from a frenetic, desperate place of trying to prove to others and myself that I, finally, am doing enough. Which is often ineffective and sometimes very harmful.

But if I settle down into the interior space of "I am enough," I not only may accomplish more, but I am less likely to cut others with the jagged edges of an ego I am trying to force on the world under the guise of "doing more." Brené Brown writes:

> Wholehearted living is about engaging in our lives from a place of worthiness. It means cultivating the courage, compassion, and connection to wake up in the morning and think, *No matter what gets done and how much is left undone, I am enough.* It's going to bed at night thinking, *Yes, I am imperfect and vulnerable and sometimes afraid, but that doesn't change the truth that I am also brave and worthy of love and belonging.*[9]

My sense of "enough-ness" is grounded in the grace of God. The Apostle Paul recounts an encounter with God in which he heard a voice telling him, "My grace is sufficient for you" (2 Corinthians 12:9). Sufficient. Enough. I used to write this verse on my arm in Sharpie marker when I felt the scary compulsion to harm myself. Now, I have it tattooed on my left forearm. Now, my arm is a palimpsest.

A palimpsest is parchment that has layers of writing on it. The older layers have been erased to make room for new writing, but the erasure is never quite complete. Evidence of the old writing remains. My tattoo ends with a semicolon, a reference to Project Semicolon, whose founder, Amy Bleul, claimed as a symbol of a sentence that could have ended but continued. The semicolon represents a story that is not over.[10]

The tattoo is on my arm permanently, in much darker ink than the white scar tissue. But the scars are still there. They are part of the story, too. The new story contains the old story. We cannot erase the

---

9. Brené Brown, *Daring Greatly* (New York: Gotham Books, 2012), 10. Emphasis in original.

10. Learn more at *https://projectsemicolon.com*.

past, only write new words, new sentences, over and in and through the older layers of our lives. My arm is a palimpsest, as is my life, as is our world, layer upon layer of story that cannot ever be completely erased or covered over. Evidence that the old words remain.

I couldn't have gotten this tattoo five years ago. I couldn't have done it, safely, if the wounds were still fresh, and certainly not if the wounds were still being inflicted. And that matters, because as a country, it often feels as if we are not only trying to erase the past, rather than writing a new story over the still-visible scars of the old, but that we are trying to write a new story while still self-inflicting the very repetitive wounds of the story we are attempting to deny. The wounds of white supremacism, racism, anti-Semitism, and patriarchy, keep being re-inflicted. I would like them to be in the past. I would like for the scars to be faded and ready to be permanently written over. But they are fresh, and red, and hurting, and that means a different type of response is needed. I want to scream at them, as I used to scream at myself, "I thought you were over this!" To end them with shame and fierce ridicule. But we are not over them. We are not. Perhaps there is still a different, more honestly and graciously true story to be written of us. So, we respond to the wounds, and we try to take away the weaponry, the blades, and we write tentative new stories, with soft markers, and it all seems like not enough, like such a paltry response to such harsh and repetitive wounding.

"My grace is sufficient for you," I wrote, over and over and over again. Sometimes it was enough to keep me from hurting myself. Sometimes it wasn't. But it was a breaking-in of something that at the time seemed so foreign to me, so impossible. Some tentative hope. Some mysterious enough-ness that I could only begin to internalize. Some kind of grace.

My arm is a palimpsest. When I look at it, I read the grace and the enough-ness before I encounter the old scars. And encounter them I must. They are a part of me, a part of my story. But they are not all of me. They are not all of my story. And they are certainly not the period at the end of my story. I have begun, tentatively, uncertainly, armed with markers against the blades, to write new stories of grace.

The direction of my internal work is turning, again, to the practices of "enough-ness." Not to indulge myself. Not as part of some sort of feel-good escapism plan. But because it's by sinking downward into that enough-ness, rather than climbing up to the peaks of "doing more," that the real work gets done. The work, not only of my own transformation, but of the transformation of the world into a true reflection of God's justice, compassion, and peace. I may not ever be "doing enough." But I can take a deep breath and remember: I am enough. And that is where to begin.

It's objectively true that there's bigger, more harmful stuff going on in the world right now than what's going on in my mind. It's just as true that the only place I have to start working toward the common good is here at home. So I will do that, faithfully, and trust that the Spirit will continue to manifest a presence for the good of all. Onward we go, one tiny act of courage at a time.

7

Sharing Stories to Change the World

I believe in the power of stories with my whole heart. I believe that learning to share our stories is central to our faith, integral to our growth together in community, and vital for doing the work of the common good. Brené Brown says the power of story is rooted in our humanity.

> We're wired for story. In a culture of scarcity and perfectionism, there's a surprisingly simple reason we want to own, integrate, and share our stories of struggle. We do this because we feel the most alive when we're connecting with others and being brave with our stories—it's in our biology.[1]

Sharing stories can break the silence enforced by oppressive systems. Sharing my own story of mental health struggle and recovery has been a way to "go first" in order to facilitate spaces where others can share theirs; while one story can break silence, more stories can create a transformative conversation.

While stories can challenge systems, systems can suppress stories. Many people are unwilling or unable to share difficult stories because of justified fears that they would lose employment, be ridiculed by colleagues, or be denied opportunities for advancement. Others have asked for help only to find access to care denied, or stayed silent because they know they have no viable options for care in their community, or have found themselves further stigmatized and marginalized by admitting their need for help. People who have experienced

---

1. Brené Brown, *Rising Strong* (New York: Spiegel & Grau, 2015), 6.

marginalization and trauma are re-traumatized when forced to share their story of pain over and over again; alternatively, people who are desperately trying to have their stories heard are simply ignored or unable to get hold of the microphone on the stage of the dominant culture.

These two realities live in tension: stories matter in the work of challenging and changing systems; and in order for people to be able to share those stories, systemic change has to happen. How, then, can the work of storytelling and the work of systemic change mutually reinforce each other? How can we facilitate communities of storytelling and advocacy—or, to say the same thing in another way, how can our faith communities be places that embrace the root meaning of the word advocacy: to give voice to the needs of a community, to call out for aid?

My work over the past several years has taken place in two primary contexts: one, the work of mental health advocacy, particularly facilitating conversations in local congregations and hospitals about ministry with those in the midst of mental health struggle; and two, as a campus minister and college chaplain. In the latter context of university and college campuses, I have somewhat inadvertently found myself on one of the frontlines of the national mental health crisis. In that context I first learned how to speak truthfully about mental health struggles, and how to co-create communities of storytelling and advocacy—communities, I believe, that are faithful to the earliest vision of what the community of Jesus-followers is called to be.

Stumbling Into Story[2]

During the same difficult time when I learned that my insurance claims had been denied, I learned from college students how to speak truthfully about my mental health struggles. Prior to checking myself in to the hospital, I had completed my first year of seminary and was scheduled to begin my internship in ministry with college students at the university next door. I had interviewed, met student leaders, and

---

2. This section is adapted from my chapter on mental health in James Franklin and Becky Zartman, ed., *Belovedness: Finding God (and Self) on Campus* (New York: Church Publishing, 2020).

even been able to attend their opening worship service before I landed back in the hospital and then left town for the residential hospital program. Once I was back home in D.C., I learned that my seminary wanted me to stay on medical leave. I was unsure when I would be able to resume classes.

My days felt unstructured. Getting out of bed was hard, especially in the gloom of my basement apartment, and it often wasn't obvious what I might be getting out of bed *for*. So, it came as a blessing to me that the campus ministry and its sponsoring congregation extended an invitation to begin working with them again in the interim. I wasn't sure what I would have to offer, since I struggled to get up in the morning, but they gave me a reason to get out of the dark apartment, and I leapt at the chance.

Well, leapt is a bit much. I sort of crawled at the chance.

As I said, I'd already met some of the students, and so I stepped into my new role as "The Intern" a little bit unsure who knew where I had been and what I had been through. It felt as though I owed some sort of explanation as to why I had shown up in August and disappeared in September, only to reappear in January. Lying about it felt, frankly, exhausting. So, at the first Thursday night worship I was scheduled to lead, I talked a bit about my experiences in my sermon. I talked about Jesus calling the disciples his friends, and about loneliness, and God understanding our lonely experiences. And I hoped that the students would know that I was okay, that they didn't have to worry about me, and that we could get back to the work of ministry together.

But that wasn't what happened. Instead, the students started coming to me, one at a time, and saying:

"I struggle with anxiety and depression, and . . ."

"I have a family member with a serious mental illness, and . . ."

"I have a friend who is going through a really hard time right now, and I'm not sure what to call it or how to help them, and . . ."

". . . and I didn't know we could talk about it in church. But now you have, so now I know we can."

And that's how college students began the long, steady process of teaching me how to tell the truth about mental health, mental illness, and faith.

As I look back, it seems to me that I stumbled into the power of story, and the power of creating space for others to share the stories they had not been sure they were allowed to share. If I had the chance, I would probably have done some things differently. It was a risky move, telling that story so soon. I've learned much since then about what is healthy for me to share and not to share, about the care I take with language, about being sure I've spent some time processing difficult experiences before bringing them into a sermon. But in all its imperfection and messiness, those first stuttering attempts to share some of my story of mental health challenges with my students opened the doorway for real conversations about the hard stuff that we all deal with.

A recent report from the American College Health Association reveals that in 2018, more than 80 percent of college students had felt overwhelmed by all they had to do, and more than 50 percent experienced feelings of hopelessness. Perhaps more telling, more than 40 percent of college students reported feeling so depressed that functioning was difficult, and more than 10 percent of students shared that they had seriously considered suicide during the past year.[3] Plenty of explanations have been advanced, both popularly and in academic research, for this crisis. The reality, of course, is a complex interaction of multiple systems and causes. But explanations aside, the campus mental health crisis is a microcosm of a society-wide reckoning with the importance of mental health and the widespread nature of mental health challenges. That's why I've found it incredibly important for students to have places to share honestly about their experiences, good and bad, struggle and celebration.

"The apostles gathered around Jesus, and told him all that they had done and taught" (Mark 6:30). I've forgotten who first pointed out to

---

3. American College Health Association, "Fall 2018 Reference Group Executive Summary," from *National College Health Assessment II* Report (Silver Spring, MD: ACHA 2018), available online: *https://www.acha.org/documents/ncha/NCHA-II_Fall_2018_Reference_Group_Executive_Summary.pdf.*

me that this short verse in Mark says the apostles told Jesus *all* they had done and taught. Read it aloud with different tones, and it means different things. Maybe they tried to outdo each other with their tales of heroic acts of faith, demon-exorcising successes, and miraculous healing. Maybe they were more honest. Maybe they talked about their failures and shortcomings. That would seem to fit the narrative, and the story following of Jesus totally bombing in his own hometown, calling the disciples at a time when his mission wasn't off to a great start, and then the gruesome execution of John the Baptist, his cousin, friend, and ally.

Imagine this gathering of Jesus's apostles—those Jesus would call his friends—sharing literally all that they had done and taught and experienced. Stories of triumphs, yes; and also stories of struggle, shortcomings, and fear. Perhaps the disciples begin as our gatherings with friends sometimes do, joking around, sharing funny stories, or humble-brags. And then someone had the courage to speak up and share a difficult story of defeat or pain. Then another, and another. Here is the earliest community of Jesus-followers gathered around a shared meal to tell stories about all they did, experienced, succeeded at, failed at. If that isn't church, I don't know what is.

Those early disciples gathered around a fire with Jesus and told stories of success and failure, doubt, and conviction. Stories of faith. Jesus, according to Mark's Gospel, invited them to come away, to rest and have a meal together. But the sharing of stories, and the retreat from the busy-ness and stress of their lives did not lead the disciples to separate themselves from the world. It created an opportunity for yet another radical form of ministry and welcome, as Jesus showed that they had plenty of food, rest, and community to go around. A gathering of friends for an honest accounting of life and ministry together became an opportunity to show God's love to the world.

That's the kind of faith community I believe we can co-create: organized around God's radical solidarity with the world in the humanity of Jesus, celebrating with each other, mourning with each other, in honest conversations about it all, and ready to go out into the world to learn, grow, feed, and serve. That's the kind of community I try to facilitate as a campus minister, by "going first" with my own story of mental health struggle to create space for others to share, and sometimes sitting back and shutting up to listen to the stories and questions and explorations of the students. When I mess up, sharing honestly about those mess-ups and mishaps becomes another chance to stumble into story together. What would it mean for faith communities to look like this early gathering of Jesus-followers, sharing stories of the good and bad of our lives, learning together in conversation?

I've lost track of how many people have told me some version of "I wasn't sure we could talk about this here"—here in church, here in faith community, here in a public place. It is powerful to say, "Yes, we can talk about that. And in talking about that with each other, we can discover ourselves, and each other, as loved and accepted by each other, and loved and accepted by God." If we can facilitate this kind of story-sharing space, we are well on our way to breaking the silence and challenging the stigma that prevents many with mental health struggles from seeking the help they need.

It doesn't necessarily take an expert to create a community of story-sharing. It does take some understanding of what makes a space safe for stories to be shared. It takes a willingness to learn, both to model vulnerability and to respect other people's vulnerabilities. It often takes someone who is willing to "go first." It takes some healthy boundaries and balance between sharing and maintaining healthy privacy, between being in it together and also being our own unique selves.

The Rev. Amy Butler offers some helpful ideas for balancing the importance of vulnerable and authentic sharing with the need for healthy boundaries:

> Thinking about self-disclosure? Here are some guidelines for measuring your judgment:
>
> 1. Sharing this moves my community to deeper connection.
> 2. I'm sharing with people who have earned the right to hear my pain.
> 3. I'm sharing from my scars, not my wounds.
> 4. I have a leadership objective in my sharing.
> 5. I can speak of my experience with humor or levity.

6. I feel confident my people can hear this without being harmed.

7. I am actively tending my own issues elsewhere in healthy ways.[4]

As we can see, modeling vulnerability means paying close attention to boundaries. Why am I sharing what I am about to share? Is this about me or about the mission of the community? Am I talking to a counselor or spiritual director about this? At the same time, this model creates avenues for an appropriate level of sharing and trust-building that are not allowed for by more authoritarian models of professional leadership.

And while different forms of ministries and different contexts call for different approaches, I have discovered a few central concepts for facilitating communities of care, story-sharing, and advocacy that resonate in ministries from college campuses to local congregations to hospital chaplaincies. I often frame these concepts for communities in terms of three tensions for pastoral care, five communal practices, and three advocacy tips.

Three Tensions for Communities

I've found that it is important for communities to be able to hold a number of different creative tensions as they enter into the work of facilitating communities where stories can be shared, healthy vulnerability modeled, and healing experienced. As I've already mentioned, in thinking about holding tension, I picture a rubber band, which does its work of holding things together by holding tension, neither completely pulling apart in two opposite directions nor collapsing into one single glob. Here are three vital tensions for faith communities to hold.

1) People with mental health struggles are both recipients **and** subjects of ministry

Many congregations begin conversations around mental health with the idea that the end result will be the creation of some form of mental

---

4. Amy Butler, "TMI," *Baptist News Global*, February 10, 2015, available online: *https://baptistnews.com/article/tmi/#.XU8hNy2ZM_U.*

health ministry that can help those in need of care. This is a noble goal, and there are many good guides that exist for congregations seeking to do so.[5] At the same time, this form of discourse at times puts the focus on ministry *to* or *for* people with mental health struggles, discounting the idea that those with mental illnesses can also be advocates, caregivers, and witnesses to the truth of the gospel in their lives and the shared life of the community. There were times in my own story where I very much needed help, comfort, and care, and other times where I longed to be able to share my own story, to hold the mic rather than being talked about or ministered to. Communities who can learn to hold this tension will be able to pass the mic to those most impacted both by the individual reality of mental health struggle and the systems and structures that create impediments to care, while taking seriously the need to provide care for those who are hurting, be it a comforting presence, a casserole, funding help, transportation, or a host of other needs.

2) Destigmatizing medication and clinical care and offering space for honest lament

Medication is complicated. Some people have grown up hearing from their faith leaders or their community that they shouldn't need medication to handle mental health struggles. Prayer and faith should be enough. At the same time, once conversations about medication have been destigmatized, medication and other forms of treatment are presented as a panacea to people in pain: "Oh, just take your medication, and you'll be fine." But psychiatric medication creates many challenges. Sometimes prescribing medication seems like a guessing game, and the patient feels like they're on a spinning dartboard with medications being thrown at them. At other times, side effects cause real problems for people. People face systemic abuses where medication is used as a means of control. And finally, the internal logic of "Just take your medication and you'll be fine" is remarkably similar

---

5. You can find some of these resources at *www.davidfinneganhosey.com/resources*.

to the logic of "Just pray about it and you'll be fine." Both are based on a far too simplistic accounting of the human experience of mental health challenge. It's important for faith communities to do the work of destigmatizing medication while also allowing space for people to be honest with their struggles with medication and treatment. Being able to hold this kind of complexity allows for caring conversations and is also good practice for taking on the complexity of the systems that prevent access to care for so many.

3) *The presence of God* **and** *the absence of God*

As I've written elsewhere, "If you want truly to understand the radical nature of God's presence, which I believe is the gospel message, you first have to come up against, and let yourself fully experience, the absence of God."[6] While our faith communities are often bad at holding this tension, our sacred texts are fantastic at it. The Book of Psalms is the most obvious example of the ability to witness to the awesome presence of God and lament the terrifying absence of God, at times in the same breath. Being able to hold this tension in community is important because it gives language to the painful experiences of mental health struggle. Beyond that, being able to honestly name the reality of hope and despair, progress and failure, is key to creating movements for change that acknowledge the full humanity of their participants. As we work to challenge and change systems, we are allowed to cry out both, "Why, O Lord, do you stand far off? Why do you hide yourself in times of trouble?" (Psalm 10:1) and "O Lord, you will hear the desire of the meek; you will strengthen their heart, you will incline your ear to do justice for the orphan and the oppressed, so that those from earth may strike terror no more" (Psalm 10:17–18). Communities that can build their tension-holding muscles will also begin developing practices for care which recognize the complexities behind these tensions.

---

6. David Finnegan-Hosey, *Christ on the Psych Ward* (New York: Church Publishing, 2018), 30.

Five Practices for Care

Here are five suggestions of practices for congregations and care teams dedicated to ministries of story-sharing and advocacy.

1) Recognizing the "two continuums" of mental illness and mental health

John Swinton writes about the two continuums of mental illness and mental health, the former being the "primary focus of the traditional biomedical narrative," while the latter "focuses on meaningful personal relationships, spiritual direction, the quest for meaning, a valued space within society, and so forth."[7] Many attempts to promote understanding of mental health in faith communities focus on the mental illness continuum, by educating pastors on the terminology of mental health diagnoses or offering basic training in mental health response to lay people, for example. These are laudable efforts that I wholeheartedly support.[8] They are of great practical use and also help to ease the worries of those who feel they do not know enough about mental illness to know how to respond. But faith communities also need to recognize, and be encouraged by, the role that we can play in the latter continuum, that of mental health. The aspects which Swinton names—meaningful personal relationships, spiritual direction, the question for meaning, a valued space within society—are very much the work of our faith communities.

Recognizing the two continuums opens the door for further practices of both care and advocacy that focus on the whole person, including their spiritual, communal, and vocational well-being. All of us have mental health. Those of us who have acute, chronic, diagnosed mental illnesses still need these spiritual practices, which makes them community unifiers rather than dividing lines. Recognizing the two continuums means recognizing that the spiritual practices of our faith

---

7. John Swinton, *Resurrecting the Person: Friendship and the Care of People with Mental Health Problems* (Nashville, TN: Abingdon, 200), 135.

8. You can learn more about Mental Health First Aid at *https://www.mental healthfirstaid.org/*, and see *www.davidfinneganhosey.com/resources* for other resources.

communities speak into the mental health needs of people with and without mental illness.

2) Presence really matters

Presence matters. Showing up matters. Accompaniment matters. This is true in the care of people with mental health struggles, and it is true in the work of advocacy as well. I often share with people that while I remember relatively little of what exactly any of my visitors in the hospital said to me, I very much remember they were there. Faith communities can practice showing up for people, whether in their congregation or in the community, even when we feel somewhat insecure about our lack of knowledge around a certain topic or situation. This is vitally important because the systems we are up against are complex; while educating ourselves and increasing our understanding matters, it is possible to get caught up in "paralysis by analysis," deciding that a certain situation is too complicated or too political to engage. We start by showing up, being present, and listening.

3) Attending to our images and metaphors for healing and recovery

I have written elsewhere in greater detail about taking care with the way we talk about healing and recovery, with the images, metaphors, and stories we choose to employ in our efforts to offer hope to those in psychic pain.[9] The story of Bartimaeus, who is "called" by Jesus to be healed, provides a powerful example. It's one of my favorite stories of vocation and calling. At the same time, the story assumes the need for a person with a disability to have a miraculous healing. This can create a story about healing that is hurtful for people with disabilities for whom wholeness looks, not like a miraculous healing, but rather like acceptance and accessibility. Paying attention to our images and metaphors also means paying attention to the way our images of healing emphasize community and the challenging of the powers that be,

---

9. David Finnegan-Hosey, *Christ on the Psych Ward*, 137–44.

rather than only emphasizing individual healing. How do the images we employ and the stories we tell lead us to challenge power and transform systems? Doing a self-audit of our favorite images of healing and recovery is an important way to practice responding to this question.

4) Affirmation isn't the same as confirmation

One of the challenges of sharing difficult stories of mental health struggles in community is that mental illness can be a liar. It can be a voice that whispers untruths about yourself, your friends, the world. It can be tempting to try to argue with the person in the midst of struggle, "That's nonsense. You're not alone. We're right here," or "That's not true. You're wonderful. Look at all these friends around you." But the person suffering may hear this well-meaning encouragement as one more fight to fight, one more undermining of their trust in themselves, or as disingenuous or dishonest.

Communities and caring individuals instead can practice affirming a person without necessarily confirming their statements about themselves or the world. "It sounds like you are in a lot of pain right now," or "You know, if I were feeling what you say you're feeling, I'd imagine that would be really scary," lets people feel heard and seen, allows for the difficult emotions and experiences of struggle to be honestly expressed, and still provides space for healing and growth to occur. This is a concrete practice of holding the tension between presence and absence, hope and despair. Someone's *feelings* can be real, and they have a loving community gathered around them whatever those feelings are.

5) Referrals as "expansions of the circle of care"

Significant strides have been taken over recent years to educate pastors and other faith leaders on the differences between their role and abilities and those of mental health professionals like counselors and psychiatrists. This is important because faith leaders often serve as gatekeepers to mental healthcare. It is still the case that a higher percentage of people in mental health crisis in the United States first seek out a pastor, clergyperson, or faith leader before they look for a mental health professional.[10] When I was in seminary, we learned a simple rule: as pastors, we were to see someone for pastoral care three times, and then we were to refer them to a specialist, to avoid falling into the trap of understanding ourselves, or portraying ourselves, as licensed mental health professionals.

It is a handy guideline, and I'm not suggesting we throw it out entirely, but I want to complexify the guidance. First, it's worth noting that this is not how we treat other forms of illness. If a student were to ask to meet with me for prayer and then began sharing physical symptoms, I wouldn't meet with them three times and then refer them. I'd ask them if they'd seen a doctor, and perhaps offer to walk them over to the student health center or, if the pain was severe, accompany them to the ER.

Second, if a congregant goes to the hospital for a physical ailment, pastors and congregations don't think their work is over just because medical professionals are involved. In fact, the faith community continues to play a role of care and accompaniment, not pretending to be medical professionals, but by being the church.

Finally, the "Three Times Then Refer" rule, while meant to protect the boundaries of the pastoral caregiver, can feel like a push-away by the person being referred. "You're too much for me to handle," or "You're too sick for us to deal with here" can feel dismissive and can inadvertently echo stigmatizing narratives about mental illness.

The Rev. Ellen Swinford, my supervisor and ACPE Certified Educator during my Clinical Pastoral Education training at the National Institutes of Health in Bethesda, Maryland, offered a helpful image that nuanced the important role of referrals in pastoral work. She asked us to imagine referrals as "expanding the circle of care" around the individual in need. I like the image because the faith community and the pastor remain in the circle of care, but other people are added

---

10. Philip S. Wang, Patricia A. Berglund, and Ronald C. Kessler, "Patterns and Correlates of Contacting Clergy for Mental Disorders in the United States," *Health Services Research* 38 no. 2 (April 2003): 647–673, abstract available online: *https://www.ncbi.nlm.nih.gov/pmc/articles/PMC1360908/*.

to complete the circle. It is good to expand the circle. The place we occupy on the circumference of the circle might be closer to or further away from the place of hurt at any given time, an idea that resonates with Swinton's two continuums. Sometimes, the mental health professional needs to be the closest to the person suffering; at other times the non-professional accompanying presence of friends, family, or the faith community may be what is needed; and at other times, questions of spirituality, vocation, or advocacy may call for a pastor, chaplain, or spiritual accompanier. The expanding circle of care acknowledges the humanity of the person hurting, the boundaries (and thus, the shared humanity) of the pastoral caregiver, and the important role that communities of faith continue to play.

Three Tips for Advocacy Work

The exact scope of advocacy work will vary from community to community and from situation to situation. Times change, communities change, and thus advocacy needs to change. Here are three tips for faith communities beginning to advocate for systemic change related to mental health.

1) Stories are important

I believe it is important for faith communities to be places where people can share hard stories. But we don't have to tell the entire story, nor even necessarily have a story of our own to share, to begin facilitating that kind of community. I spoke with a pastor whose congregation had begun a community-organizing effort by holding a series of listening sessions in their neighborhood. The topic of mental health kept coming up, and it was clear to the pastor and the congregation that some action was needed, but they were unsure how to proceed. The pastor began naming people with various mental health challenges in the prayers of the people during their Sunday service.

"So one week I prayed for people experiencing depression," the pastor told me, "and the next week for people experiencing anxiety, and then a third week for people with bipolar disorder." As the pastor named "people with bipolar disorder," I choked up with tears. Though, at this point, I was quite comfortable sharing my story of mental health struggle, it was still powerful to hear myself named and recognized in prayer within a faith community that was not familiar with my story. A simple (and communally shared) practice like the prayers of the people can be a place to begin creating a space where people feel seen and heard, and feel safe and empowered to share their stories, which is important in and of itself and can serve as the basis for organizing and advocacy efforts.

2) Make the links to systems clear from the beginning

Even as we begin facilitating story-sharing space, we need to start making the links with broader, intersecting conversations around the mental healthcare system, access to the system, and medical debt. Congregations can build relationships with organizations that are already making these connections well. The Poor People's Campaign, for example, is already describing the links between medical debt, a broken healthcare system, systemic racism, and a matrix of other interlocking systems that conspire to keep people poor. RIP Medical Debt, which buys unpaid medical debt and then forgives it, is happy to work with churches to raise money for this cause: a $1 donation can forgive $100 of medical debt, which makes it a low-bar entryway for churches, who are often motivated, first, by a direct response to need, and then can be introduced to the deeper systemic and policy dynamics behind that need. We can draw those broader, systemic connections at the same time as we begin the work of story sharing, which in turn creates confidence that stories are not being shared in a vacuum, but in the midst of work to make the world a safer place for the story-sharers to live.

3) Honor the humanity of those involved in the work

As we engage in advocacy work, it is important to do so in a way that honors everyone involved as human, made in the image of God, and part of the common good. Faith communities can take the lead in ensuring that movements are trauma-sensitive and balance activism with healthy contemplative and spiritual practices.[11] When we march out of the doors of the church we do so as vulnerable humans, not as invulnerable automatons—that's what Jesus came to show us.

Our humanity matters in this work, for we are part of the common good. By acknowledging that at the beginning of our work, we make the movement for systemic change in mental healthcare accessible even to those who themselves struggle with mental health. Since we all have mental health, at one point or another in our lives all of us struggle with it.

Mental Health Voting

It is not lost on me that this book is being published in the same year as possibly the most closely watched election in United States history. In fact, I began writing this book just as conversations about the 2018 midterm elections were heating up, and there was much talk about healthcare and pre-existing conditions. I voted in 2018 with a high degree of awareness of the way in which that election would impact my and millions of others' access to care, as someone with a pre-existing condition and who, in the past, has had to rely on Medicaid expansion to cover mental healthcare costs.

But what does it mean to vote for a better mental health system? The National Alliance on Mental Illness (NAMI) has good issue-specific information on their #Vote4MentalHealth website,[12] but their focus tends to narrow on policy that directly relates to mental health. As I hope this book has made clear, many other systems impinge on the mental health of individuals and the health of our society. Here, then, are a few ideas for what to keep in mind when voting with a more just and equitable mental healthcare system in mind.

---

11. I'm grateful for the work of Teresa P. Mateus and the Mystic Soul Project, this intersection of trauma sensitivity, spiritual practice, and activism: *www.teresapmateus. com/* and *www.mysticsoulproject.com/*. An accessible introduction to some basic practices for trauma sensitivity is her book *Sacred Wounds: A Path to Healing from Spiritual Trauma,* published under Teresa B. Pasquale (St. Louis, MO: Chalice Press, 2015).

12. *www.nami.org/Get-Involved/Take-Action-on-Advocacy-Issues/Vote4MentalHealth.*

Vote to protect coverage for pre-existing conditions and parity in coverage for mental health.

Any attempt to repeal or dismantle the ACA without a viable replacement that protects pre-existing conditions harms people with mental health struggles. Currently, the federal government has joined with twenty states to argue in federal court *against* these protections, while at the same time allowing for healthcare plans that lack such protections and also lack mental health parity,[13] another issue that the ACA was designed to address. Mental health voters should challenge these attempts to return to the discriminatory policies of the past at both federal and state levels. To be clear, it is possible to propose an alternative to or replacement of the ACA that addresses these concerns; but absent such an alternative, the repeal of the ACA would lead to a vast gap in coverage for people with mental health conditions.

Vote to expand Medicaid.

As I mentioned earlier, I relied on expanded Medicaid to access mental and physical healthcare during a crucial time in my recovery. Many people with mental health struggles lack the resources to access care; the expansion of Medicaid, while not a magic fix, would provide coverage for millions more people including people with mental health struggles. Importantly, many people with disabilities rely on Medicaid in order to be able to live in their own homes and remain connected to their communities, a nuance that is often lost in conversations about the Medicare-for-All models. If private insurance were to be replaced by a universal Medicare system, it would be important to argue for and maintain the aspects of Medicaid that are uniquely related to disabilities.

---

13. "NAMI and Others File Lawsuit against the Short-Term, Limited Duration Plan Final Rule," *NAMI*, September 14, 2018, available online: *https://www.nami.org/About-NAMI/NAMI-News/2018/NAMI-and-Others-File-Lawsuit-Against-the-Short-Ter*.

*Refuse to let mental health struggles be used
as a scapegoat for difficult political conversations.*

Too often, politicians are willing to talk about mental healthcare because mental illness is being raised as the "real issue" in order to avoid difficult political conversations around guns, extremism, gender, and race—in spite of the fact that people with mental illnesses are much more likely to be victims, rather than perpetrators, of violence. Mental health voters are willing to have a robust conversation about the importance of mental healthcare in creating a safer society for all, *without* allowing people with mental health struggles to be used as scapegoats by politicians who, often, turn out not to be serious about the conversation around mental healthcare.

*Recognize that homelessness and mass incarceration
have taken the place of a functioning mental health
system in our country.*

It's clear that deinstitutionalization, while originally designed to end abuses and put more of a focus on care in community, has actually, when paired with budget cuts to healthcare and community programs, led to homelessness and an increase in mass incarceration. Mental health voters will pay close and critical attention to rhetoric around homelessness, incarceration, and crime, knowing that often these conversations demonize people who are struggling with mental health and trauma.

*Recognize that tax cuts for those with the most means
losses in care and services for those with the least.*

Related to the last point, we will pay close attention to budget cuts—often hidden under language about tax cuts—that continue to make it difficult for people to receive the care they need, whether in a psychiatric bed or in a community setting.

Recognize that behind headlines about drug overdoses and the opioid crisis are stories about mental health struggles, substance abuse disorders, and trauma.

We ought to be talking about the public health crisis of opioid addiction, just as we previously ought to have talked about crack cocaine in terms of public health rather than crime. We ought to be talking about it in terms of underlying causes such as substance-abuse disorders, trauma, and mental-health struggles. If politicians are seeking to use the opioid crisis to bolster their campaigns but aren't talking about increasing resources for care and recovery while decreasing punitive measures and homelessness, we should raise questions. And if they're doing so while also talking about cutting taxes for those with the most, we ought to remind them those tax cuts mean losses in care and services for those with the least.

Refuse to shame or demonize people whose voting behavior is different from their own.

I think it is important to vote with the mental healthcare system in mind. I also think we shouldn't shame or demonize people who don't vote, or who vote differently from us, especially when we're talking about mental health voting. For some people with severe mental illness, getting to the polls is difficult under normal circumstances, much less in a time in which voting rights are being eroded by voter ID laws, the closing of polling places, and the purging of voter rolls. Rather than criticizing those who don't vote, we must vote with them in mind and help to cast an inspiring vision that can catch the hopes and interest of those who have stayed home out of disengagement and disinterest in past elections. Those of us with mental health struggles ought to understand, more than anyone, that feelings of disengagement and disconnection can be truly powerful, and that shaming and demonizing language, far from motivating us, tends to drive us deeper into the corner.

Obviously, there are many more aspects of this conversation to consider, but these are a few topics I've noticed rattling around in the political sphere. If you are able to vote, consider these thoughts about mental health voting. The more we tell our stories, the more the system will have to change. The more the system changes, the more people will be able to access care. The more people are able to access care, the more sacred stories we will be privileged to hear. And we need to hear those stories. Gathered in a circle, around a shared meal, in the presence of Christ, we share our stories, and then we are sent out in the world to love and to work for the common good. Because planted within those stories are the seeds of real change.

CONCLUSION

And Grace Will Lead Us Home

I have a confession to make. I didn't want to write this book. I knew it needed to be written. I knew that expanding the conversation around mental healthcare in our faith communities is one of my callings in life. But I didn't *want* to have to write this book.

My encounters with the mental healthcare system have been complicated, and at times difficult. To delve into the most painful aspects of those experiences is challenging; to broaden the exploration into some of the most broken and oppressive aspects of our system is harrowing. Of course, exploring such brokenness is not as painful as experiencing it directly. In many ways I have been buffered against the worst harm of the brokenness of our mental healthcare system, but second-hand trauma is trauma nevertheless, and writing this book has often felt like a spiritual struggle, perhaps, against the very "powers of the air" to which the author of Ephesians so cryptically refers.

Writing this book has been hard. But I knew I needed to write it because of all of the stories I have heard as I have traveled over the past few years speaking in church fellowship halls and hospital conference rooms and college auditoriums and private living rooms and the back rooms of pubs: stories of frustration and hurt, of lack of access to care, lack of parity, lack of equity, lack of justice. I have heard the stories, and I have heard the hard questions that I haven't been sure how to answer, but which call for a response.

One of the most common questions, often preceded by the story of a friend or a family member who is suffering but who seems to refuse offers of support, has been, "How were you able to reach out and ask for help?"

It's one of the most difficult questions for me to answer. The truth is that I'm not sure. I know it is not because of any heroism, or virtue, or strength, or moral superiority that I have and others don't. I'm a better person for having asked for help, but it wasn't because I'm a better person that I could ask for help. If you have lost someone in your life due to mental illness, as I have, you know that it's an awful, awful thing, and that no answer or explanation can make it less awful. So I try to respond in a way that avoids creating any sense of shame or guilt. There's so much we don't know, don't understand, and don't control about suicidal behavior. In writing and talking about it, I hope to push back against shame, stigma, and silence and help more people get help. But when someone is hurting so badly, it just hurts. And the words I have to offer seem so limited. Three things helped me to ask for help, and one thing made it harder. The three things that helped were people in my life who talked about their mental health struggles with me; people who checked in on me when I was having a difficult time; and access to care. The thing that made it harder was the toxic constructions of masculinity. Let me share just a little bit about each of these.

First, people in my life talked about their mental health struggles with me. This started with my family. My father and mother both worked to break through the generational pressure of family secrets and talk to me about the histories of mental illness, addiction, and compulsion in their families. At the time, it probably made me uncomfortable, and I probably didn't know what to do with it. But when I hit a real crisis point in 2011, I had some groundwork laid, some vocabulary, some dim understanding that mental health struggles existed in my family, and the awful experience I was having might not be an isolated incident, but a part of a larger whole. That helped me reach out for help.

Second, people checked in on me when I was having a difficult time. Friends noticed that something was up, and they asked about it. I didn't always know what to say to them. Sometimes, I flat out denied anything was going on, but the cumulative impact of people asking if I was okay helped me ask for help. This is important: even if it seems like you're not getting anywhere by checking in on someone, it helps. I wasn't always ready to respond, but when I eventually did reach out, I was enabled to do so by the support that had already been shown to me.

Third, I had access to care. I wasn't as aware of this as I am now, but I had a level of access to mental healthcare that is often denied to people in this country. I had a ride to a hospital. I had people around me who not only knew how to get me to the hospital but knew what I needed to tell the ER staff so that I could get help. I had economic resources and buffers (though even with them, I ended up in massive debt). I had a generally positive view of healthcare, that hospitals were a thing that were there for me and there to help me. For many people, barriers to care mean barriers to asking for help. If I'm going to encourage people to share their stories, push back against stigma, and ask for help, I also need to be working to change unjust structures so that when people do ask for help, they can get it. Otherwise, encouraging people to share their stories and ask for help isn't helpful; it's even a little bit cruel.

And one of the structures that needs to change in order to ensure better access to care is the toxic way we construct masculinity. Even in a family that had worked hard to talk about mental health and mental illness, I still picked up on the subconscious message that men shouldn't cry. And that we should be careful about how long we hug other men. If we continue to teach boys and young men that crying is bad, that talking about feelings is bad, that violence is the only acceptable way for men to express emotion, how are boys and men going to reach out for help?

More broadly, we teach people in general that being able to do things on their own is the most important virtue, that independence and individual strength matters most, that asking for help and needing help are weaknesses. This messaging seeps in through the cracks of our societal facades and makes it much harder for people to share difficult stories and to seek help.

Why was I able to ask for help? Ultimately, I don't know. It was an experience of grace; and yet, again, I don't think the difference between me and those who can't or won't or don't ask for help is that I have grace and they don't. Grace, however hidden, is available to those who are hurting badly. I believe that deeply. I also believe there are ways for us to be means of grace for each other in a way that leads to more health and wholeness. We can do so by talking honestly about our mental health struggles. We can do so by checking in on people we are connected with when they seem to be struggling. We can advocate for just and equitable access to mental healthcare. And we can teach and model healthier understandings of gender, of masculinity, of our need for each other, of the interdependent realities of our existence as humans. And our faith communities can be places where we do all of these things, where we can truly experience each other as means of grace in a community of grace.

Amazing Grace

One of the most familiar Christian hymns of all time, "Amazing Grace," was written by John Newton, an English priest who had formerly been involved in one of the sickest systems the world has ever seen, the transatlantic slave trade. The song emerged from Newton's own conversion experience, which led him to quit the slave trade. He sought to actively repent of his past by becoming an abolitionist and allying himself with William Wilberforce, the member of Parliament who led the charge to abolish the slave trade in Britain. Hidden in the background of a hymn that seems to be an ode to the most personal dimension of grace is a testimony to the social consequences of God's gracious activity in the world. When President Barack Obama sang "Amazing Grace" at the conclusion of his eulogy for the Rev. Dr. Clementa Pinckney, the pastor of Mother Emanuel AME Church in Charleston, South Carolina, who was shot and killed along with eight parishioners by a white nationalist during a weekday Bible study, the social context of the hymn was highlighted and added to. President Obama ended his remarks about Pinckney, and the others killed, by both singing and quoting the hymn.

> He knew that the path of grace involves an open mind—but, more importantly, an open heart. That's what I've felt this week—an open

heart. That, more than any particular policy or analysis, is what's called upon right now, I think. . . . If we can find that grace, anything is possible. If we can tap that grace, everything can change. Amazing grace. Amazing grace. . . . Through the example of their lives, they've now passed it on to us. May we find ourselves worthy of that precious and extraordinary gift, as long as our lives endure. May grace now lead them home.[1]

I've often thought of this old hymn, made new again in so many different contexts, in writing these pages. I have thought, in particular, of a line from the second verse:

'Twas grace that taught my heart to fear, and grace my fears relieved.

To face the brokenness and pain of our mental healthcare system is a fearful and often discouraging task. And yet it is an act of grace to be made aware of the ways in which we fall short, individually and communally, of God's full vision of the healing and wholeness of all of creation. It is grace that teaches our heart to break at the things that break God's heart. And it is grace that acts in our lives and in our world to bring healing of that heartbreak. It was grace that made me fear tackling this project, that continues to make me cognizant of the weight of the matters at hand. And it is grace that relieves those fears. It is all grace. "From his fullness we have all received," as John's Gospel says, "grace upon grace" (John 1:16). Amazing grace.

It is my prayer that this book is a means of grace for you. That it has challenged and encouraged, troubled and comforted you as it has, in the process of writing, done for me. That it has broken your heart open rather than breaking it apart. That it has left room for you to step into the big, bold, conversation of many stories and many voices that we must have if we are to see change in the way we treat people with mental health struggles in our faith communities, in our country,

---

1. President Barack Obama, "Remarks by the President in Eulogy for the Honorable Reverend Clementa Pinckney," *Office of the White House Press Secretary*, June 26, 2015, available online: *https://obamawhitehouse.archives.gov/the-press-office/2015/06/26/remarks-president-eulogy-honorable-reverend-clementa-pinckney*.

and around the world. I pray that you have encountered the grace in this book, which the author of Ephesians says will save us, will heal us, will bring us, finally, to that place where it is the Prince of Peace, rather than the "Ruler of the Power of the Air," who orders the systems within which we interact and relate and grow and change. Bring us to that place which is our true home, the very heart of God.

Grace, I have tried to say throughout this book, is the pre-existing condition of all creation. It was there long before us. God's very act of creation was an act of grace, and God continues to infuse all of that creation with grace even as the brokenness of human-invented systems strives to impede its free-flowing transformative power. Grace saves, heals, and liberates us *from* the reality of broken systems and *for* the work of caring for the common good, a goodness which precedes all of the hurt and all of our own striving. In the midst of sharing difficult stories, of caring for each other and ourselves, and of struggling against the powers and principalities which prevent people from finding the healing and wholeness for which they were created, grace remains. Sometimes it is a quiet whisper in our hearts. Sometimes it is a shout from the mountaintops. Grace came before us. Grace is here with us. And grace, finally, will lead us home.

Resources for Action, Advocacy, and Care

In the fall of 2019, more than seven years after my last hospitalization for bipolar disorder, I once again found myself in the position of needing to admit myself to the hospital for my own health and safety. The experience was a reminder of grace—both the grace of a time of relative tranquility and peace and the grace made manifest in the care of friends, family, faith community, colleagues, and mental health professionals. It also reinforced for me the way that the institutions that make up this country's mental healthcare and heath insurance systems operate as powers and principalities, often organized around the maintenance of control rather than care. And it renewed my commitment to improving access to care, including by making sure more people have resources for action, advocacy, and care. What follows is only a partial list of resources; an updated list, along with a free discussion guide for this book, can be found at *davidfinneganhosey.com/resources*.

If you or someone you know is in a crisis, you can call the National Suicide Prevention Lifeline: (800) 273-8255. The lifeline now also has an online chat option: *suicidepreventionlifeline.org/chat/*.

You can also reach the Crisis Text Line by texting HOME to 741741.

For LGBTQ+ Youth: The Trevor Project provides phone, chat, and text support. Call (866) 488-7386, text (202) 304-1200, or click here for the website: *www.thetrevorproject.org/get-help-now*.

For transgender individuals: The Trans Lifeline offers support for transgender people by transgender people. Call (877) 565-8860 in the United States or (877) 330-6366 in Canada, or click here for the website: *www.translifeline.org/*.

For veterans: Call (800) 273-8255 and then press 1; text 838255; or click here for online chat: *www.veteranscrisisline.net/get-help/chat*.

You can also research whether your community has a Mobile Crisis Unit which can respond to mental health emergencies.

If you or your congregation wants to be better trained to respond to mental health crises, check out Mental Health First Aid trainings in your community: *mentalhealthfirstaid.org*.

Many organizations exist to advocate for various aspects of a more just and equitable healthcare system in general and/or mental healthcare system in particular.

The Poor People's Campaign organizes nationally around issues that intersect with poverty and a more just economy, including healthcare: *poorpeoplescampaign.org*.

RIP Medical Debt aims to cancel billions of dollars of medical debt: *ripmedicaldebt.org/*. They were originally founded out of Rolling Jubilee, which now focuses on other forms of debt relief: *rollingjubilee.org*.

The National Alliance on Mental Illness has mental health voter information at *nami.org/vote4mentalhealth*, as well as faith-based resources at *nami.org/namifaithnet*.

While I don't always agree with their policy positions, the Treatment Advocacy Center is a good resource for information on psychiatric beds and the criminalization of mental illness: *treatmentadvocacy center.org*.

Many denominations have established mental health initiatives. The United Church of Christ has an office for Disabilities and Mental Health Justice, with excellent resources for congregations and leaders: *ucc.org/disabilities_and_mental_health_justice*. The Christian Church (Disciples of Christ) has a Mental Health and Wellness Initiative through their National Benevolent Association: *nbacares.org/mental-health*. In addition to denominational resources, many ecumenical organizations have identified health and wholeness as programmatic priorities. For example, the North Carolina Council of Churches's Partners in Health and Wholeness program focuses on health topics including mental health and addiction: *ncchurches.org/programs/phw/*.

TRACC (Trauma Response and Crisis Care) for Movements is a new, national organization dedicated to training trauma-aware caregivers in support of social movements: *tracc4movements.com/*.

This is by no means a complete list—more resources can be found at *davidfinneganhosey.com/resources*. If something has been particularly helpful for you that isn't on my website, I would love to hear about it: *https://davidfinneganhosey.com/*contact.

Thank you for reading, and thank you for sharing stories to change the world.